"Finally a practical guide to addressing diversity in the workforce—not just on the obvious topics of gender and race, but on other differences and how those who are in the minority feel when confronted by attitudes and preconceived notions in the workplace."

—Roxanne Decyk, Vice President, Corporate Planning, Amoco Corporation

"I found this book highly readable. In the current business climate, it's not easy to develop and manage human resources effectively—these authors show how it's done. Real people make their pages come alive. I recommend *Workplace Diversity* to all managers who believe that a top-flight workforce is an organization's most precious asset."

—Christopher Lovelock, international management consultant, educator, and author of
Product Plus: How Product + Service = Competitive Advantage

"User friendly. Well written—a most helpful tool for managers and supervisors."
—Juliet F. Brudney, "Living with Work" columnist, *Boston Globe*

"*Workplace Diversity* fits an unmet need for a manager's guide to diversity. It should become part of the reference materials in every orientation program for new managers."

—David A. Thomas, Associate Professor,
Organizational Behavior and Human Resource Management, Harvard Business School

"*Workplace Diversity* is one of the most useful management books I have read. Quite clearly, the authors' purpose was to help managers on the firing line deal constructively and positively with one of today's most difficult challenges. And I believe they have succeeded. The whole tone of the book is warm, supportive, and human. It reflects a true understanding of the pressures on middle management caught in the cross current of down-sizing, profit goals, legal requirements, social pressures and backlash, and their own concerns for security and growth. It offers sound, understandable advice on specific, frequently encountered issues in honest, straightforward language. I enthusiastically recommend it."

—Avram J. Goldberg, Chairman, The Avcar Group, Ltd.,
and retired Chairman and CEO, Stop and Shop Companies, Inc.

"This is an excellent resource for the ordinary manager who is working with a diverse group. It is well organized, well written, and can be used for general learning on diversity as well as for insight on dealing with specific questions."
—Judith D. Palmer, Regional Diversity Coordinator, Procter & Gamble

"*Workplace Diversity* offers an innovative approach to understanding diversity practices. Full of facts, cases, and practical discussion, it is an entirely down-to-earth guide for those who are serious al   ness approaches diversity."
—Laura M. Gold, Director of Di   tion

D1365402

WORKPLACE DIVERSITY

Published by
Adams Media Corporation
260 Center Street, Holbrook, MA 02343

ISBN: 1-55850-482-6
Printed in the United States of America

First Edition
J I H G F E D C

Library of Congress Cataloging-in-Publication
Esty, Katharine C.
Workplace diversity: a manager's guide to solving problems and turning diversity into a competitive advantage / Katharine Esty, Richard Griffin, and Marcie Schorr Hirsch.
p. cm.
Includes bibliographical references.
ISBN 1-55850-482-6
1. Diversity in the workplace. 2. Personnel management.
I. Hirsch, Marcie Schorr. II. Griffin, Richard. III. Title
HF5549.5.M5E85   1995   95-7926
658.3'041—dc20   CIP

This publication is designed to provide accurate and authoritative information with regard to the subject matter covered. It is sold with the understanding that the publisher is not engaged in rendering legal, accounting, or other professional advice. If legal advice or other expert assistance is required, the services of a competent professional person should be sought.
—From a *Declaration of Principles,* jointly adopted by a Committee of the American Bar Association and a Committee of Publishers and Associations

This book is available at quantity discounts for bulk purchases. For information, call 1-800-872-5627 (in Massachusetts, call 617-767-8100).

Visit our home page at http://www.adamsmedia.com

WORKPLACE DIVERSITY

Katharine Esty, Richard Griffin,
and Marcie Schorr Hirsch

Adams Media Corporation
Holbrook, Massachusetts

ACKNOWLEDGMENTS

WITH gratitude to all of those who have assisted, supported, and borne with us.

Thanks to Jill Kneerim for her belief in this book and its message and to Richard Staron at Adams Publishing for his help and guidance throughout the process.

Thanks to Jeanne Connerney, Anne Quintal, and Anne Tornow for their thoughtful editorial assistance, research, and word processing. Special appreciation to Allison Cobb for her beyond-the-call-of-duty research and graphics.

Thanks to the many colleagues who took a role in the development of this book, beginning with the "Voices" project group, and our readers who generously shared their expertise in reviewing parts of our text. They include Patti Benowitz, Jane Bermont, Cindi Bloom, Jeanne Connerney, Kim Cromwell, Michael DiIanni, Gil Dubé, Katie Herzog, Ajit Maira, Laurie Margolis, Thomas O'Connell, Joseph Perkins, Linda Perruzzi, Anne Quintal, Nancy Scanlon, Stephen Shestakofsky, James Spencer, Nancy Stout, Larry Stybel, Liandro Barros Viana, and Gil Williams.

We take responsibility for the information presented and the opinions expressed, but we truly appreciate our colleagues' infusions of insight, wisdom, and practical ideas along the way!

And, of course, enormous gratitude to our families, friends, and colleagues for their patience, good humor, and love.

Katharine Esty
Richard Griffin
Marcie Schorr Hirsch
Cambridge, 1995

TABLE OF CONTENTS

READ THIS FIRST!

HOW TO USE THIS BOOK

This is a desktop reference tool. Keep it handy in your office, and refer to it whenever diversity issues arise.

Read through the list of chapter headings to see the range of material covered. Because of overlapping implications, some issues may be covered in more than one section. (For example, the chapters on parents and women cover some of the same issues.) If in doubt, check both.

The format below has been used in each chapter. Subheadings clearly mark each section of the chapter.

- *The Subject* gives an overview of the topic of the chapter from its historical context to key issues and particular areas of sensitivity in the workplace today.

- *The Law* briefly describes the relevant legal information you must know in order to deal with the subject in a manner consistent with the latest employment law thinking.

- *Common Issues and Concerns* presents the problems most frequently encountered by managers and supervisors.

- *Working Examples* offers mini-cases that we have heard in our consulting work that may be similar to the workplace dilemmas that you face.

- *Questions and Answers* offers a selection of queries about each topic in workplaces today.

- *Action Steps that Work* suggests proactive initiatives that supervisors and managers can take to head off difficulties in the future.

- *Gaining Competitive Advantage* is a quick checklist of do's and don'ts to turn the quandaries posed by diversity into pluses for your organization.

A list of resources—organizations, books, articles, and audiovisual materials—for further assistance related to the chapter topic is included at the conclusion of each chapter. There is also a general reference section at the end of the book.

Introduction

My workgroup looks like the United Nations. There are guys
from Taiwan, India, and Mexico. Two of the women come from
the Philippines. In fact, there are only two people in the whole
group who were born in America. Just ten years ago there were
only white guys. Managing was a piece of cake because we
were all like family. All that's different now. Every day there is
a new problem. With the incredible mix of people, it's not sur-
prising. It feels like a whole new ball game to me, but it sure isn't
baseball or any other game I've ever played.
—NICK MOAKLEY, A MANAGER IN A MIDWESTERN FACTORY

Today's workforce is truly a mosaic of different races, ages, genders,
ethnic groups, religions, and lifestyles. As a manager or supervisor, it
is your job to ensure that disparate pieces of the mosaic fit together in
a harmonious, coordinated way, maximally utilizing the talents and
abilities of each employee. If skillfully managed, this diversity can
bring a competitive advantage to an organization. If not, however, the
bottom line can be negatively affected, and the work environment
can become unwelcoming.

Dealing with a diverse workgroup is new terrain for most managers and supervisors. The United States rose to the top using a one-
size-fits-all approach to managing employees. This worked in the past
because, historically, most of the workforce was white, and male. This
has all changed. No other country in the world rivals the incredible
diversity that we see in the United States. This means that we can't
turn to other places or earlier times for models of how to manage
diversity. And, because few received training in managing diversity at
school or college, supervisors and managers must learn about diversity on the job.

There are two important managerial challenges posed by diversity:

Challenge number one: Managers must deal with the day-to-day problems that arise when people in their workgroups speak different languages, come from different cultures, espouse different values, or have totally different life experiences. They must cope with the issues that develop when a workgroup is made up of people unlike themselves and one another in terms of race, gender, age, ethnicity, sexual orientation, religion, family situation, and place of birth.

Challenge number two: Managers and supervisors must learn how to create a work environment in which diversity and difference are valued and in which all employees can contribute to their fullest potential. If both of these challenges have been successfully met, your organization will have a competitive advantage over most others. Failure to meet either of them will diminish your workgroup's productivity and mark you as lacking one of today's most critical managerial/supervisory skills. In the future, few organizations will be able to afford those who cannot work successfully with diverse employees. *In brief, the ability to manage diversity is a fundamental requirement for managers in the 1990s and will continue to be important for the foreseeable future.*

Many companies have recognized that the workforce is changing and want to help their managers deal efficiently with diversity. Unfortunately, as many organizations are now recognizing, edicts from the CEO and other "top-down" policy statements do little to assist the managers and supervisors on the front line. Another common approach has been to provide diversity awareness training to all managers and supervisors. These programs can work well in alerting supervisors and managers to the sea change that is taking place. But a one-shot awareness program cannot begin to provide all the answers to the slew of questions that will arise in the workplace—new questions each day—each requiring understanding and skills.

It is you—the managers and supervisors—who are really on the diversity frontier. *Workplace Diversity: A Manager's Guide to Solving Problems and Turning Diversity to a Competitive Advantage* is written for you. This is the book to keep on your desk to refer to as new issues confront you. *Workplace Diversity* will serve as a primer, a guidebook to assist you.

From our work as consultants to a wide range of organizations from Phoenix to Providence, from Seattle to Savannah, we have learned that most managers and supervisors have good intentions. But *good intentions are not enough*. Even when managers and supervisors want to create a work environment in which everyone feels appreciated and valued, it's just not that easy to do.

Diversity poses complex questions. For example, what is fair? Is it fair to treat employees who are different exactly the same? Or is it fairer to treat them differently, according to their needs? Government regulations about equal opportunity and affirmative action have generated dozens of such questions and dilemmas that never existed in the past. They have been instrumental in creating opportunities for many employees; at the same time, a powerful backlash has been unleashed in their wake.

No Easy Answers

What is politically correct (PC) and what is not, is a major debate today. We believe that the concern about political correctness can create the impression that all we are talking about is language and terminology. This book doesn't offer guidelines for political correctness. We also do not believe that a rigid set of rules will be helpful. This is because the rules are changing rapidly, even as we write. But also, we think that managing diversity goes far beyond finding a correct term for someone who is different or eliminating a word that somebody finds offensive. It involves changing our entire work culture.

We will help you think through the problems you are facing in your workplace. If there is a tried-and-true answer or solution, we'll tell you. And where there is no single right answer, we'll tell you that, too. We will provide you with a road map, giving you the right questions to ask, options to think about, and several solutions to consider.

This book is organized to be user-friendly. We are aware that you probably have a thirty-six-hour job to do in a twenty-four-hour day. For easy reference, we have written chapters on major dimensions of diversity: gender, race, ethnicity, age, religion, sexual orientation, parental status, disability and hierarchy and class. As you face a problem, you can quickly turn to the appropriate chapter. In each chapter, we'll tell you what the law says and summarize the most common issues and concerns. We'll analyze several problems that are frequently encountered, we'll respond to questions we've been asked in our consulting work, we'll provide you with some do's and don'ts, and we'll list resources if you want to dig deeper into the topic. To sum it up, we have created a no-frills, no-nonsense guide to help you get through the jumble of management jargon and politically correct babble and come up with good solutions to the dilemmas that a diverse workforce can create.

Most importantly, the suggestions made in this book can be implemented by you as a manager or front-line supervisor. Of course, it is our hope that, ultimately, entire organizations will become sensitive to the diversity of their workforce and change policies and practices to better support it. Right now, however, the reality is that many organizations are not there. At present, most organizations have a diverse workforce, but, at the same time, they have procedures and policies that are more or less out of date.

You are probably not trying to reengineer your whole organization anyway. As a contemporary supervisor or manager, you are trying to cope with a changing work environment, and you may be finding that the tried-and-true ways of managing don't quite fit. Mostly you just want to get the work done. It is for you that this book was written.

CHAPTER 1

THE DYNAMICS OF DIVERSITY

A ONE-MINUTE HISTORY

When an eighth-grade class in Concord, Massachusetts was studying immigration, one assignment had students find out where each of their four grandparents had been born. It turned out that twenty-five of the twenty-six eighth graders had one or more grandparents born outside the United States. This example underscores what most of us were taught about the United States: It is a country of immigrants, a melting pot of diverse peoples.

Traditionally, the metaphor of the melting pot has suggested that Americans start out as diverse, differentiated entities, but that as a result of continuous exposure to one another over time, a "meltdown" occurs and differences tend to disappear. The slogan E Pluribus Unum—"one from many"—suggests this same theme.

ASSIMILATION

In the typical workplace of the nineteenth and early twentieth centuries, managers saw themselves as helping in the meltdown process of diminishing differences. It was a common assumption that assimilation was the goal—i.e., assisting those who were different to become more like the people already in the workplace or, more exactly, more like the people in power. For years, this goal of assimilation was taken for granted. Expressing differences through dress, language, perspective, customs, practices, or values was discouraged. People responded by Americanizing their names, shedding their ethnic dress, attending night school to learn English, and working hard to become part of the American dream.

Some differences, however, such as age, race, gender, and sexual orientation, could never be eliminated, even with effort or night school. Eventually many people realized that they did not want to abandon their cultural heritage, their religious practices, or their uniqueness.

Judith Palmer, in her 1989 article "Diversity: Three Paradigms for Change Leaders,"[1] outlines three ways in which diversity in the workplace has been viewed. She states that the way many people in the past have dealt with diversity is to see it as a moral issue. They attempt to create opportunities for people who are diverse because it is the just, fair, and right thing to do. She calls this paradigm "The Golden Rule."

A second paradigm, which she labels "Righting the Wrong," focuses on dealing with diversity as a legal issue. From the beginnings of the civil rights and feminist movements, large numbers of people became more aware of the injustices wrought upon people of color and women. In the 1960s and 1970s, affirmative action (AA) and equal employment opportunity (EEO) legislation was passed. Many managers in workplaces across the country struggled to comply with the law and to treat everyone the same. Although the creation of the "protected classes" did lead to increased opportunities for many diverse workers, these laws also created a backlash. Many people were convinced that affirmative action was actually unfair because the effort to undo past wrongs often entailed treating people in the present unfairly; quotas became a dirty word.

Palmer's third paradigm is "Valuing Diversity." Here the goal changes from assimilation to valuing the differences that exist. This involves increasing the awareness of differences among employees and appreciating the value these differences add to the organization.

In this third paradigm, the goal is not necessarily to change people, but to change the organizational systems and culture so that the organization can become inclusive and move from being monocultural to being multicultural.

This third paradigm represents a major departure from the typical assumptions of many managers and supervisors, such as the idea that treating people exactly the same is the fairest approach. Giving people what they need if they are to be employees who contribute fully means treating different people quite differently. The idea of giving up the goal of assimilation, however, is still unsettling to some of today's managers.

Diversity is clearly a fact of the American workplace. There is

---

[1] Judith Palmer, "Diversity: Three Paradigms for Change Leaders," *Journal of the OD Network*, March 1989.

much work to be done before each manager and supervisor understands what valuing diversity means for him or her on a day-to-day basis. In the remainder of this chapter, we describe some of the dynamics of diversity; that is, we look at what happens in organizations to people who are different. Having described the dynamics and some of the perceived problems associated with diversity, we then talk about the benefits of workplace diversity and how diversity can become a competitive advantage.

WHAT IS DIVERSITY?

In this book, we have chosen to focus on ten dimensions of diversity that we believe are the most critical for the workplace. (See Figure 1.1.)

We do not include in our definition a host of other ways in which people differ, such as intelligence, personality type, physical beauty, or what they do for hobbies or fun. The dimensions we have selected may create identity groups or cohorts—visible and invisible. Most people find that several of these dimensions have particular meaning for them. For example, two of us (Katharine Esty and Marcie Schorr Hirsch) are particularly attuned to issues of gender and family, while another of us (Richard Griffin), because of his life experience, is more focused on the dimensions of age, disability, and religion. When we are not the same as the majority of other people in the workplace setting, we tend to notice our membership in the less numerous group.

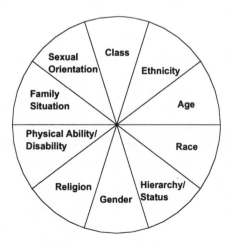

Fig. 1.1 Workplace Diversity: Key Dimensions

For example, Katharine, as a woman on a management team with six men, was aware of being a woman. As the working mother of two, Marcie is often aware of work and family issues.

Most books on diversity in the workplace have dealt with these differences as if they all had the same impact. We think the issues involving each one are somewhat different from those of the others. Being a person with a disability is not the same as being an Orthodox Jew among Protestants or a Filipino in a company whose employees are primarily of Irish and Italian descent. However, there are some common dynamics that run through many of the dimensions, and that's what we describe in the rest of this chapter. The ten chapters that follow will discuss some specific and unique problems of each dimension.

Xs AND Os: INS AND OUTS

In a landmark video and book called *The Tale of O*,[2] Rosabeth Moss Kanter explains that in every workplace there are two kinds of characters, Xs (the people found in large numbers) and Os (the people who are scarce, different, few in number). What happens in most organizations, Kanter argues, is that the Os stand out and get special attention. Notice how your eye is drawn to the O here:

The Os typically feel that they are walking a tightrope. Even a small mistake may be disastrous to them. Kanter's *Tale of O* also describes a number of other consequences of being an O. Os are frequently asked to be on every task force that is formed because each group needs an O, and there aren't that many to choose from. Often Os are asked to speak for all the Os in the organization: "What do you think about this issue?" Os are usually most noticed for their "O-ness,"—their differences—, and their skill or competence may go unobserved.

---

[2] Rosabeth Moss Kanter, *The Tale of O, On Being Different in an Organization*, New York: Harper and Row, 1980.

This video, which was produced in the 1970s and revised in 1993, has sold more than 1 million copies and has been translated into forty languages. It captures, in a fanciful and deceptively simple way, the basic dynamics that are set into play by the person in an organization who is different.

"A Class Divided," a PBS documentary with Judy Woodruff that appeared on Frontline, demonstrates other dynamics—those of discrimination. In 1970, in Riceville, Iowa, a third-grade teacher named Jane Elliot decided to teach her class a lesson on discrimination. On the first day of her experiment, the children with blue eyes were given special privileges, such as getting seconds at lunch and extra time at recess. The brown-eyed children were required to wear a large collar. Jane Elliot made ongoing comments such as, "Blue-eyed children are smarter than brown-eyed children" and "Blue-eyed children learn faster than brown-eyed children." Within half an hour, the blue-eyed children started calling the brown-eyed children names and treating them as inferior. The next day she switched roles. The brown-eyed children became the superior group and received the privileges, while the blue-eyed kids had to wear the ugly collars and lost their recess.

This video dramatically illustrates how discrimination can be created very swiftly. When the authority, in this case the teacher, treats one group with privilege and respect while denigrating the others, it is only a matter of minutes before the Ins begin to treat the Outs the same way. In the film, you see the Out group children become depressed; they seem to wilt as you watch. Most important of all, the test scores of whichever group was Out dropped sharply.

In our diversity training programs, we use both *The Tale of O* and *A Class Divided* to stimulate awareness of the dynamics of diversity. Following the video, we ask participants to reflect on a time when they have felt like an O in the workplace or to describe to their table a time when they felt like an Out. We then ask them to tell the story about that time and, in particular, to remember what they felt when they were an O or an Out and how they behaved.

Below are two lists generated by participants in several recent diversity training sessions.

How I Felt as an O or an Out

Angry	Stressed
Depressed	Out of place
Isolated	Cautious
Frustrated	Uncared for
Low self-esteem	Special and unique
Sad	Disrespected
Lonely	Invisible
Resentful	Uncomfortable
Incompetent	Inferior
Stymied	Confused

How I Behaved as an O or an Out

Pulled back
Stopped trying
Lost my ambition
Left the situation
Did the least possible, worked to rules
Focused on things outside work
Performed less well
Didn't take any risks
Tried harder
Was silent
Closed down

IMPACT OF FEELING LIKE AN O OR AN OUT

It does not take much of an imagination to see that if people in the workplace are feeling depressed, isolated, disrespected, etc., they tend to pull back or cease trying, and their performance will be negatively affected as a result.

Regardless of which particular group an employee identifies with, the dynamics of power in organizations cause everyone to experience feeling In or Out in much the same way. From our focus groups and surveys in organizations worldwide, we have learned, in fact, that many people in the workplace feel like Os and Outs. Of course, not everyone in a given group feels this way, but a sizable percentage do.

This includes people who are different along every dimension of diversity in our definition:

Men and women
People of color
People from various cultures
People with certain religious practices
Older and younger workers
Gays, lesbians, and bisexuals
People from differing class backgrounds
People at different levels of the organization
Workers with significant family responsibilities
Foreign-born individuals
People with disabilities

It is important to note that our definition of diversity is itself inclusive. We feel it is important in diversity work not to create an us versus them kind of dynamic. For example, we have found that white men, especially older white men, can often feel like Outs. So can people who look like the majority but have an unseen disability or are gay. When you look at your workgroup as a whole, it is certainly possible that a number of its members are feeling like Os and Outs. As a result, they may be working far below their potential. Their performance may be unnecessarily reduced, and their productivity may be down.

CLUSTERED AT THE BOTTOM
People who are different, who are Os or Outs, are frequently clustered at the bottom of the organization and tend not to advance as fast or as far as others. This is partially due to the feelings and behaviors we have just described that are generated by being an O or an Out.

But there is more to the story. Those at the top of the organization, managers and supervisors, play a key role. Managers see Os or Outs and say to themselves such things as:

"They really don't want the responsibility."
"They prefer a lower-level job."
"They aren't ready for advancement."
"It would be too risky to promote them."
"They don't seem serious about their careers."
"They aren't qualified for the job."

What is not so evident is that almost everyone who feels stuck in an organization soon starts to behave like an O or an Out. Sooner or later, he or she looks unmotivated and not very competent. What often isn't recognized is that this is not a quality in the person, but a consequence of feeling like an O and an Out.

Given more opportunities to learn, to grow, to take on challenges and responsibilities, an individual may look very different. As a manager or supervisor, before you decide that anyone is unpromotable, explore the possibility that what that person needs is more opportunity and more challenge.

"Old-boyism" and the Like

The principle of social similarity in social psychology states that, given a free choice, people tend to pick people just like themselves to work and associate with. In organizations, this is particularly true at the top of the corporate ladder, where jobs entail huge responsibility. Managers tell us that they select people they can trust to do the job the way they themselves would do it. The fact that the people they choose tend to look just like them is purely coincidental, they claim.

At Ibis, for example, a women-owned firm, we found in our early days, as we started to grow, that we were drawn to hiring women who were our friends, whom we had worked with before, and who we knew shared our values. They also looked just like ourselves, despite the fact that we were working in the diversity area and wanted to diversify the staff. It took consciousness of our bias, and frankly, an enormous effort, to take the greater risk and hire some men and some people of color. This experience with the "old-girl network" gave us an understanding of some of the complexities of "old-boyism" and developed our empathy for dealing with it in other organizations.

Problems with Diversity

A lot is being written about valuing diversity. What is rarely mentioned, however, is the long list of problems reported by people who are actually dealing with diversity in the workplace. In this book we recognize that there can be issues with diversity, and that managers will need guidance and assistance in dealing with them. Here is a sampling of the kinds of problems that managers and supervisors report to us in dealing with diverse workers:

Feedback
Discipline
Quality and performance
Communication
Timeliness and absenteeism
Accuracy
Schedules and deadlines
Initiative and risk taking
Teamwork
Interpersonal conflict
Terminating a poor performer

In short, these are all problems that managers typically encounter every day with nondiverse workers. However, when an employee is visibly different from coworkers in one or more dimensions, a manager can have a hard time knowing for sure whether the problem is one of diversity or just an ordinary management issue. Is he or she coming down too hard or not hard enough? It gets blurred. And because the person is "not like me," the manager's natural confidence in dealing with the issue can sometimes disappear. It can be harder. It can take more time. It can take more effort, but it is usually worth it.

DIVERSITY: A COMPETITIVE ADVANTAGE

This brings us back to the most fundamental question: Why is it worth it? Why should a manager or supervisor work toward increasing diversity and creating a work environment in which diversity is valued? The most important answer to this question is that valuing diversity will help your organization's bottom line and give your organization a competitive advantage. Here are some of the ways in which well-managed diversity can be a competitive advantage:

1. *Increased productivity.* In a workplace in which people feel respected, included, and valued, they will stop acting like Os or Outs and productivity will go up.
2. *Fewer lawsuits.* In 1993 the EEOC extended the "hostile environment" standard to workplace bias based on age, race, religion, disability, color, or natural origin. Lawsuits cost corporations and other organizations enormous amounts of money, to say nothing of time and energy lost. For example, the Lucky

Stores grocery chain settled a gender bias case for $107 million in April 1994. In a workplace in which diverse workers are respected and truly valued, there will be fewer suits.

3. *Retention of business.* A number of organizations now pay careful attention to the demographics of companies with which they do business. In particular, federal agencies and municipal governments have taken the lead in saying no to prospective suppliers and clients who cannot demonstrate a clear commitment to diversity. For example, a midwestern city refused to buy computer equipment from a high-tech company whose sales team was entirely white.

4. *Increasing marketing capabilities.* A diverse employee group can provide insight into the thinking of a wide range of customers. As markets become more differentiated, the smaller market segments become more important. Attracting new customers can be the critical difference between survival and going out of business.

5. *Creating the largest possible talent pool for recruitment.* In this day of increased competition, it is important for every organization to hire smart, energetic people and to have access to the largest possible pool of talent. Any company that smacks of "old-boyism," where what you see at the top of the house is primarily white males, may find itself at a disadvantage. At the very least, it may find that a high proportion of the talented candidates who are women and people of color will choose other organizations.

6. *Becoming an employer of choice.* The word spreads like wildfire about which companies are the best for women, for people of color, for people with disabilities, for gays, etc. The grapevine also spreads information about which companies are known to be tough places for parents, for women, for blacks, etc. Sometimes it is only when a company learns that it has a bad image that it is ready to change. For example, one Big Eight accounting firm in an eastern seaboard city usually hires about twenty new accountants every year. In 1993, nine women turned down the firm's offers and accepted jobs at its major competitor. The women explained that they had learned that the second firm was known to be a good place

learned that the second firm was known to be a good place for women, with lots of flexibility regarding work arrangements and generous parental leaves.

There are at least three more benefits to be gained by having a diverse workgroup, although these benefits are harder to measure and quantify than most of those mentioned above.

BETTER MORALE

Employees who work in organizations that are totally homogeneous, say all white or all men or women, frequently tell us that as the workplace becomes more diverse, the ambiance becomes more lively. For example, when an all-male school became coed, the presence of women faculty and female students brought a number of changes. There were more celebrations such as birthday parties, less hazing, less sarcasm, and even, it was reported, fewer broken windows. A number of faculty reported that morale had never been so good—even at exam time.

HEIGHTENED CREATIVITY

The creativity experts tell us that creativity is fostered in settings where people come from a variety of backgrounds and differ from one another along many dimensions. Task forces usually draw their memberships from many levels and many functions and often have greater diversity of gender and race than their organizations as a whole. They are therefore typically extremely successful in coming up with solutions to long-standing problems. When the whole workgroup, business unit, or organization is diverse, creativity may bloom.

IMPROVED DECISION MAKING

The decision to go ahead with the invasion of the Bay of Pigs in Cuba was made by a group composed entirely of white men. Social psychologist Irving Janis, who coined the term *groupthink*, believes that decisions are improved when the decision-makers come from a variety of different perspectives.[3] We wonder whether the invasion might have turned out differently, or whether it would have taken place at

---

[3] Irving Janis, *Victims of Groupthink: A Psychology of Foreign Policy Decisions and Fiascos*, Boston: Houghton Mifflin, 1972.

all, if there had been several women, a number of Hispanics, and some disabled war veterans included in the planning process.

Diverse groups have the potential for making high-quality decisions because they must deal with dissenting views before they move forward.

DOING WHAT'S RIGHT

Most people believe in social justice and equal opportunity. Many people feel good about increasing the diversity of their organizations. They believe that an inclusive organization is more just than an exclusive organization. They want to create workplaces in which every person can contribute to his or her fullest potential. When they understand what this means for them day to day, they are willing to do it. When they do it, they feel good about themselves and their organizations.

That is what this book is all about. Helping you, the managers and the supervisors, understand what you can do day by day to solve the problems that diversity may present to you and how you can turn diversity into a competitive advantage.

CHAPTER 2

WOMEN—GENDER

THE SUBJECT

MORE women! The biggest change in the workforce in America in the last twenty-five years has been the dramatic increase in the number of women. Most of the women joining the workforce have been between the ages of twenty-five and fifty-five. Today there are more than 55 million women in the labor force in the United States, or some 46 percent of the total. (See Figure 2.1.) In fact, 55 percent of women are working outside the home today, and this percentage is expected to continue to rise. (See Figure 2.2.)

> "The growing number of women in the labor market is probably the most important development in the American labor market that has ever taken place."
> —DAVID E. BLOOM, LABOR ECONOMIST, *OPPORTUNITY 2000*, HARVARD UNIVERSITY, P. 19

More than thirteen million women will have been added to the workforce between 1986 and the year 2000, including significant numbers of African-American, Hispanic, and Asian women. It should be noted, however, that being active in the workforce is nothing new for African-American women—their participation rate has traditionally been considerably higher than that of white women. (See Figure 2.3.)

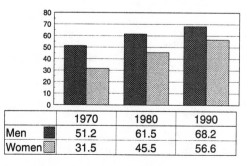

	1970	1980	1990
Men	51.2	61.5	68.2
Women	31.5	45.5	56.6

Fig. 2.1 Numbers of Women and Men In the Workplace (in millions)
Source: U.S. Bureau of Labor Statistics.

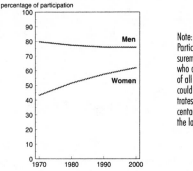

Fig. 2.2 Comparison of the Participation Rates of Women and Men in the Labor Force
Source: U.S. Bureau of Labor Statistics.

Progress for working women, however, has been uneven. Women continue to earn only 77 percent of what their male counterparts earn, and fewer than 7 percent of the most senior executive positions in corporations are held by women. Typically women move in and out of the workforce far more frequently than men—to have children, to care for aging parents or a sick relative, to move with their husbands, etc. According to one recent study, women who leave the workplace experience a 33 percent drop in wages when they return, and their pay never catches up again.

Today 62 percent of temporary workers and 67 percent of part-time workers are women. This means that most of the jobs that have fewer benefits, lower rates of pay, and less security are held by women. For all these reasons, it is important to continue to pay attention to women in the workplace.

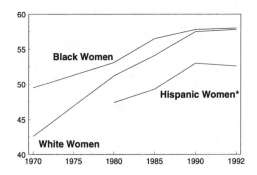

Fig. 2.3 Participation Rates of Women in the Workplace by Race
Source: U.S. Bureau of Labor Statistics. Statistics nor available before 1980.

BUSINESS WEEK'S BEST COMPANIES FOR WOMEN

Pacesetters	Up-and-Comers
Avon	American Express
CBS	Baxter International
Dayton-Hudson	Corning
Gannett	Honeywell
Kelly Services	IBM
US WEST	Johnson and Johnson
	Merck
	Monsanto
	Pitney Bowes
	Security Pacific Bank
	Square D

Business Week, Aug. 6, 1990.

The situation of women in the workplace is starting to change. A number of companies, such as U S WEST, Avon, and Gannett, are making enormous strides toward being more supportive of women. For example, Avon launched an effort back in 1977 to promote saleswomen out in the field. It hired consultants to help change corporate culture to be more supportive of women, sent women to management development programs, and provided on-site child care. By 1990, 27 percent of the officers were women.

"It's not that the world would have been better if women had run it, but that the world will be better when we as women, who bring our own perspective, share in running it."
—BETTY BUMPERS, CONFERENCE SPEECH, 1985

Some women complain that they are stuck at lower and middle levels, and others describe their work environments as difficult and uncomfortable for women. They talk about a "glass ceiling," a "backlash," and a "stalled revolution." Others see a much rosier picture and believe that women in the workplace are making remarkable progress in terms of increasing their numbers in positions of power and responsibility and widening the range of careers and professions open to them. (See Figure 2.4.) The flood of women into the workforce has increased the awareness of difficulties for those with significant family responsibilities. We will cover these in more detail in Chapter 9 entitled "Parents—Work and Family."

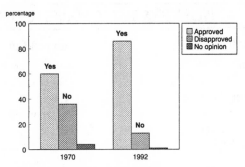

Fig. 2.4 "Do you approve of a married woman holding a job in business or industry if her husband is able to support her?" *Gallup Poll Question, 1992*

"Real equality is going to come not when a female Einstein is recognized as quickly as a male Einstein, but when a female schlemiel is promoted as quickly as a male schlemiel."
—BELLA ABZUG

A note on the words *sex* and *gender*. We use the word *sex* to refer to biological characteristics and physical differences between males and females. *Gender*, on the other hand, refers to the roles people play and how men and women are perceived to differ in the social context.

THE LAW

Title VII of the United States Civil Rights Act of 1964 prohibits discrimination in the workplace on the basis of race, color, gender, religion, or national origin. It is a violation of Title VII to refuse to hire or promote someone because of gender stereotypes or preferences of coworkers, clients, or customers. Stereotypical comments about and behaviors toward women can be seen as gender bias and can lead an organization into years of costly litigation.

It is also unlawful to label jobs as "men's jobs" or "women's jobs" unless gender is a bona fide occupational qualification (BFOQ). For example, the Supreme Court recognized gender as a BFOQ when it allowed prison officials to select only males for guard jobs in maximum security prisons. Title VII covers most employers with fifteen or more employees. The federal Equal Employment Opportunity Commission (EEOC) has issued guidelines that assist in interpreting the letter and spirit of the law.

The Equal Pay Act of 1963 gives men and women the right to earn equal pay for doing "substantially equal work." At the time this law was passed, women were earning sixty-three cents for every dollar men were earning. The Civil Rights Act of 1991 was enacted in the wake of several Supreme Court rulings that made it more difficult for victims to prove discrimination. The act expands the kinds of employer conduct prohibited by federal antidiscrimination law. It also entitles employees charging intentional discrimination to jury trials and, in appropriate circumstances, to recover punitive and compensatory damages. As a result, employers' potential liability in such cases and the cost of settling complaints have increased.

In a 1993 case, *Harris v. Forklift*, the Supreme Court provided additional guidance on what constitutes a sexually hostile environment. In that case, Teresa Harris, a former employee of a truck leasing company in Tennessee, quit her job at Forklift Systems, Inc. The president of the company had made repeated crude remarks and sexual innuendos, even after she complained and he promised to stop. After a trial, a lower court ruled that Harris could not prevail without establishing that the president's behavior caused her psychological injury.

On appeal, the Supreme Court rejected the need to show psychological injury to prove sexual harassment. The Supreme Court ruled that in order for a work environment to be determined to be sexually hostile, the totality of the circumstances must be considered, including the frequency and severity of any discriminatory conduct and whether it unreasonably interfered with the employee's work performance or was merely an offensive utterance.

COMMON ISSUES AND CONCERNS

In our consulting work in the last decade, we have talked with thousands of women in hundreds of workplace settings. Whether we are in a manufacturing plant, a bank, or a government agency, there are four or five issues that are mentioned over and over again.

PUT-DOWNS AND DISRESPECTFUL COMMENTS

Some women in the workplace tell us that they face a stream of offensive comments. They describe crude remarks about their bodies and their appearance. Often they face intrusive questions such as, "How was your weekend? Did you get laid?" Many women tell us that dirty jokes and off-color comments make them uncomfortable. Even terms of endearment, such as "honey" or "dearie," are offensive to growing numbers of women at work. While workplace cultures differ greatly, from more formal organizations such as banks or law firms to more casual workplaces such as factories and foundries, the issue of disrespectful language exists everywhere to some degree.

OUR COMMENT

The dilemma for the supervisor and manager is that individual women differ dramatically in their reactions to comments. Some women tell dirty jokes themselves with great gusto, while others feel uncomfortable when a man remarks, "I like your sweater." What this means is that you must check out the reactions and concerns of the particular women in your workgroup. Ask them from time to time if anything is causing them discomfort. There is no way to find out how they are faring without asking. Remember, some women, in their eagerness to fit in or to advance, never complain, no matter how upset they feel. It is your job to be sure the work climate is not a hostile one and is one where women will not be afraid to voice their complaints.

> "We must stand in a new posture, walking with a loving heart, an open mind, and a very big stick called clout. If we do that, we can live to see the start of the Egalitarian Era: a reality in which women become something there is no word for—that is, not unequal by virtue of gender."
> —NAOMI WOLF, *FIRE WITH FIRE,* P. 52

Preferred Words According to Five Diversity Consultants

Woman instead of *girl, gal, lady, chick, doll, broad, bimbo, female*

Person power instead of *manpower*

Chair or *chairperson* instead of *chairman*

People or *humankind,* instead of *man* or *mankind*

To staff or *to operate* instead of *to man*

Words Likely to Offend

honey, sweetie, dear, love, sweetheart, darling, baby, baby doll

Questions Likely to Offend

Is it that time of the month?

Did you get any last night?

WHY CAN'T A WOMAN BE MORE LIKE A MAN?

The management style that is considered desirable in many organizations is a command-and-control, John-Wayne style of decisive action. Others describe it as a kick-ass-and-take-names style. This style is assumed to be effective in getting the work done. Women, who frequently have a different management style, may be labeled weak or indecisive. Judy Rosener, in her article, "Ways Women Lead,"[1] calls the style that is typical of most women "interactive leadership," because the manager is focusing on every interaction with others.

Women tend to:

- Encourage participation
- Solicit input
- Share information widely
- Share power
- Seek to enhance the self-esteem of people they work with

Ironically, when women do display the command and control style, they are often criticized for it. They are labeled "too aggressive," "tough broads," "real bitches," or "iron maidens." In other words, what is seen as positive behavior in a man may be evaluated negatively in the woman manager or supervisor.

OUR COMMENT

Don't judge style, judge results. Beware of stereotypes and old-fashioned thinking about roles for women. Successful women use a variety of styles effectively, and all managers need the latitude to develop a style that works for them. Help the women who report to you to develop such a style. They may need feedback from you to understand what works for them and what doesn't.

WOMEN = INVISIBLE

Women often tell us that they feel invisible at meetings, particularly when there are few other women present. One woman puts it like this: "I make a point, but no one reacts. The next speaker goes back to the last comment made by a male. I feel like I am not being seen, not being heard. It can make you crazy—and over time it makes you

---

[1] Judy B. Rosener, "Ways Women Lead," *Harvard Business Review,* March–April, 1992.

hesitate to speak." At the same time that their comments are ignored, women may find that their appearance and clothing get a lot of attention. To have your comments about the task ignored and, at the same time, to be told you have nice legs can be infuriating.

OUR COMMENT
Research about women in the workplace indicates that women are, in fact, more frequently interrupted than men and that their comments are more frequently ignored. Watch out! This is subtle sexism, and it often passes unnoticed by managers and supervisors. If you observe a woman's comments being neglected, you can say something like, "I want to get back to Jessica's comment; no one reacted to her point, which I feel is important." Or say, "Jessica, please repeat what you just said." Once you are on the lookout for it, you may be amazed at how frequently women are ignored.

STUCK IN THE MIDDLE
Despite progress, large numbers of women have not yet reached the highest echelons of organizations. For example, in 1993, fewer than 7 percent of corporate directors or officers in the Fortune 500 companies were women. Most senior management positions are still held by white men. In years past, this seemed natural, as there were few women in entry-level and middle management positions. But women have now been in the workplace for decades; nearly 50 percent of managerial and professional jobs are held by women, yet the number of women at the top is still small.

OUR COMMENT
The old boy's network is still thriving. This network of social relationships is a major reason why women don't move as fast as men or rise as far. It works like this: Women don't play golf with the men in positions of power as often as men do; they don't have lunch with the top executives; they don't usually sit on boards with men. This lack of social contact reduces the chance that a woman's name will come to mind when senior managers fill top-echelon positions.

"Whatever women do they must do twice as well as men to be thought half as good. Luckily, this is not difficult."
—CHARLOTTE WHITTON

Take a look at who you have been promoting over the last couple of years. Do they include people different from yourself in race, gender, ethnicity? While it is natural to be most comfortable with people exactly like yourself, you need to be sure you are looking at the full range of talent. Usually this means that you have to go out of your way to find candidates who are different from yourself.

A second major reason for women's slower advancement is that many women have two jobs—a job at work and caring for children and a household on their "off hours." Bradley Googins and Dianne Burden of Boston University found in their research study that, on average, women with children were working a total of eighty-four hours a week at their jobs and at home, while men with children were working an average of sixty-eight hours.[2] Some women refuse jobs with increased responsibility because they want to have time at home with their children. And some men don't see women with small children as potential material for jobs with increased responsibilities. (See Figure 2.5.) The real problem comes when managers make this assumption and never even ask.

SEXUAL HARASSMENT

This, of course, is not exclusively a women's issue. In fact, we see sexual harassment as primarily an issue of power. The vast majority of incidents, however, do involve women being harassed by men, usually by men who are higher up than they are in the ranks of the organi-

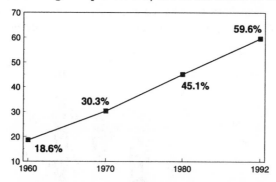

Fig. 2.5 A Growing Percentage of Married Women with Children under 6 Years Are Working
Source: U.S. Bureau of Labor Statistics.

---

[2] Bradley Googins and Dianne Burden, "Vulnerability of Working Parents: Balancing Work and Home Roles," *Social Work*, July–August 1987, Table 1, p. 297.

zation. The power differential makes the less powerful person easy prey. (See Figure 2.6.)

No organization is immune from sexual harassment. In our diversity audits of major companies across the United States, we always hear examples of behaviors that might be characterized as sexual harassment. This is true even in companies with a policy in place, and even when the organization has a history of responding quickly to any complaints about harassment. The impact of sexual harassment incidents can be significant—both on the employee and on the organization.

OUR COMMENT

As a supervisor or manager, you may well find that training for your staff is a good place to begin to address the issue of sexual harassment. Having a complaint process that is widely understood is also important. The goal is for employees to feel comfortable confronting situations at an early stage, where a win/win solution is possible. But because these situations are uncomfortable, some managers just look the other way. If you feel uncertain about how to handle a complaint, go to Human Resources and ask for help. Here are a few reasons why women hesitate to speak up about sexual harassment.

WORKING EXAMPLES
IT'S A MAN'S JOB (GENDER-BASED JOB ASSIGNMENTS)

At a plastics factory in New Jersey, it is customary to hire men to operate all the machines and to hire women as quality inspectors and

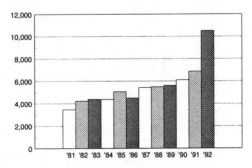

Fig. 2.6 Numbers of Sexual Harassment Cases Filed with EEOC
   Source: Equal Employment Opportunity Commission.

EFFECTS OF SEXUAL HARASSMENT

On the Employee

Loss of concentration
Shame, anger
Depression
Anxiety
Days out of work
Attorney fees
Counseling fees
Loss of job

On the Organization

Hour spent in investigations, meetings
Lower morale
Loss of loyalty
Damaged reputation
Absenteeism
Lower productivity
Legal fees
Employee turnover

for clerical jobs. A woman named Diane Koslowski has approached the company and applied for a job operating one of the complicated machines. Paul Gentile, the plant manager, thinks Diane is the best candidate, but he knows that all the machine operators see operating a machine as a "man's job," and that they will give him a very hard time if he goes ahead and hires her, to say nothing of giving Diane a rough time.

OUR COMMENT

Some workers cling to stereotypes about women and what is "women's work." When he consulted us, we encouraged Paul to hire

WHY WOMEN DON'T SPEAK UP

Ignorance—of the law, of company policies, of one's rights as an employee

Confusion—lack of understanding about what caused the behavior

Doubt—mistrusting one's perception of the behavior

Concern for others—not wanting to "make the situation public" or to hurt someone's feelings

Fear—of not being believed

—of feeling humiliated or somehow blamed

—of being ostracized by coworkers

—of damaging or losing career

—of a long, drawn out battle where the outcome is unknown

Diane. But Paul needs to realize that in order for Diane to have a chance at being successful, she will probably need extra support, extra training, and ongoing feedback. We suggested that Paul meet with the men who operate the machines and explain exactly why he is going to hire Diane. He needs to ask for their support, and he needs to give them specific ways they can help Diane get off to a good start. The men will probably keep a distance from Diane, and without a formal process to help train her on the job, she may well fail.

A TOUCHY SITUATION (UNWANTED TOUCHING)

Lori O'Brien, who works as a secretary in an insurance company in Iowa, has a problem with Joe Searson, a vice president. He started dropping by to chat with her a few months ago. After a few weeks, he began patting her on the back or shoulders as he kidded around. Lori didn't know what to do, so she laughed. Now, she tells us, he comes by almost every day and has continued to touch her on the back, shoulders, and arms. Lori has finally told her supervisor, Tiffany Keilor, about her problem. But she says she doesn't want to hurt Joe's feelings. Tiffany cannot understand why Lori didn't speak up sooner.

OUR COMMENT

Tiffany must take action. She should urge Lori to tell Joe directly to stop the behaviors she finds offensive. Lori could say, "Stop touching me!" If Joe doesn't stop immediately, Tiffany needs to help Lori. She might speak to Joe herself, saying, "This is a serious problem." If this second step still doesn't work, Tiffany should call Human Resources. Supervisors and managers must understand that it is part of their job to listen to and to act upon these kinds of complaints. Lori's supervisor, Tiffany, needs to be sure that the situation is resolved—to do nothing may put the company in jeopardy of a lawsuit, as well as produce long-lasting negative effects on Lori.

THE CUSTOMER WITH GENDER BIAS

Jennifer Steffian works for an accounting firm in San Diego. She brought a major account into the firm several years ago, and the account has grown significantly. Recently Jerry Bradley, her manager, got a call from the client saying, "Although Jennifer has done a good job, we would like a change of account manager—in fact, we'd like a man to replace her."

OUR COMMENT

This is a tough one. First of all, if it is really just a case of wanting a man on the job, that is an unlawful request. Some people have been trained to think that customer service means agreeing to everything a client or customer requests. They assume that Jerry will have to go along with what the client wants. We think that it is not that clear, and that some information needs to be gathered before any decisions are finalized. First, Jerry needs to talk to the client, listen to that side of the story, and hear in-depth what the issues and concerns are. If it is a performance problem, Jerry needs to discuss the matter with Jennifer and, perhaps, call for a problem-solving session with Jennifer and the client. If it is a case of gender bias, Jerry will need to take this problem to his manager to learn about company policy and how he should proceed. If Jerry does go along with the client in this case, the company could face a discrimination lawsuit.

QUESTIONS AND ANSWERS

Q: I am a marketing manager in a company that makes a variety of consumer goods. While my boss, Jack Stephenson, is very encouraging and respectful to me as a woman, he tells me that I should let my assistant manager go because she's too mousy and is incompetent. "Besides," Jack adds, "your image is being hurt by having her as your assistant." I see her quite differently—as bright, talented, and productive. How do I handle this?

A: We suggest that you provide a series of opportunities for Jack and other high-level managers to see your assistant's work first-hand. Be sure her name is on the reports she writes, and give her credit for projects she does on her own. You might also want to consider sending her to a leadership training program. If your company has a formal mentoring program, find her a mentor. In short, give her opportunities to show her stuff, give her access to people at higher levels, and offer her developmental experiences. But stay open to the fact that you may be in error in your assessment. Develop objective criteria to measure her effectiveness.

Q: I have just moved to a new state and am looking for a job. A week ago, I found out that I am pregnant. Do I need to tell this to potential employers?

A: The legal answer to this question is No. You may feel you are not being entirely up front if you do not mention it; however, mentioning it is definitely a risk. Some employers will certainly decide to hire someone else if they know you are pregnant. If you don't tell your new employer until you have been hired, it may be a little sticky for you, but it is an acceptable way to handle it.

Q: In my company, a small distributor of British products, the president, a rather formal Englishman, walks around the building at six o'clock every night shaking hands and chatting with each of us. My hours are nine to five in theory, but everyone stays until the nightly "grand rounds" are over. I want to pick up my daughters from day care by 5:30, but I realize that if I leave, the president will get the impression that I am cutting corners. I am very serious and have good prospects for advancement, as I am in charge of half of the contracts for the company. Should I stay late or not? I've usually finished what I need to do by five o'clock.

A: Unfortunately, many managers still measure competence by "face time," that is, by the number of hours put in at the work site. While a few pioneers are moving toward measuring competence by the quality of work, this is still fairly rare. It sounds as if you stay until six only for show. We suggest that you think of some alternative ways of chatting with the president. You need to consider talking with your boss, as well, and getting his or her view on your problem. We wonder if the president understands the kind of pressure his nightly tour is putting on his employees.

Q: I am a white man who has been passed over for promotions twice. Both times a woman got the job. I think it's because of affirmative action and quotas, and it makes me furious. What should I do?

A: We suggest that you go to your manager and ask for a meeting to discuss why you were passed over. Tell him or her that you want very specific feedback and that you want to learn exactly what it will take for you to get the promotion. It may be that your organization is trying to promote women, but it may also be that there are other factors more related to your individual performance. You need to find out. Ask whether there are affirmative action goals or not.

Q: I'm the director of human resources for my company, and I'd really like to see women move into senior positions in our organization. Although I hate to make this old cliché more credible, I really can't find women in our organization who have the right experience for these upper-level jobs. I'd like to encourage promotion from within, and I'd like our women to get a fair crack at these positions. But right now there doesn't seem to be a way to make this happen. Any ideas?

A: In a survey done by Catalyst, a research organization in New York City, 90 percent of senior managers said that line experience was critical or important to advancement. However, women are far less likely than men to be in such jobs. This pattern begins early, when women gravitate to staff positions that require credentials (such as law) as a means of combating antifemale prejudice, and continues as they seek staff opportunities to capitalize on their interpersonal skills. Clearly, to develop a pool of female talent in-house, you must be proactive. Job rotation programs can be a good step to ensure that women get the experience they need; working with junior women to guide and assist them in planning their career paths and providing them with appropriate training opportunities can help ensure that you will have a diverse pool of talented employees for senior-level openings that occur in the future.

Q: Several really sharp women work for me in my department, and they should have bright career prospects in our organization. I'd like to encourage their development, but I'm flat-out busy. I don't even have the time to coach employees, let alone serve as a mentor for a half dozen of them. Will they just have to make it on their own?

A: There are many things besides individual career coaching or mentoring that you can do to support the development of your female employees. One effective strategy is to bring selected employees along to important meetings or presentations. This gives them important visibility and exposes them to varied issues. Making sure that you request ample funds for training at budget time is another non-time-gobbling effort that you can make on behalf of your employees. Once you have the funding, you can send them to conferences and professional seminars and provide other appropriate training opportunities to ensure that they are prepared for future opportunities when they arise.

Q: I manage a group of employees who are engaged in telephone sales. I am a woman; all of my salespeople are male. One of my employees consistently sprinkles his calls with terms like "sweetie," "honey," and "babe." Mike is among my most successful people, and I have yet to hear a complaint about his choice of words. But I still feel uncomfortable about his language. Should I let sleeping dogs lie?

A: We don't advise it. Just because people aren't bringing complaints to you doesn't mean that they aren't offended; in addition, you don't know what business you are losing when Mike simply turns people off and they go elsewhere for their purchases. You need to establish protocols for acceptable language in all areas (not just about women) and articulate them clearly to your group. Salespeople represent the company, and its image can be severely damaged by unprofessional, inappropriate communication.

Q: I'm one of a half dozen department directors who were hired by the new president of a medium-sized insurance company when he came on board eighteen months ago. Last year I had my second child, and I negotiated with the president to reduce my previous full-time schedule to a four-day workweek. Last month, the president announced the promotion of all the other directors to the vice-presidential level; I was the only one of our group not promoted. I think I've been identified as being on the "mommy track" and I'm furious. What's my best next step?

A: We have seen numerous situations in which bosses assume that employees who are also mothers don't want the responsibility, long hours, or travel of higher-level positions, and mentally take them out of the running; in other cases, there is a policy excluding part-time employees from higher management positions. Once you've cooled down, meet with your boss to determine the criteria for this last round of promotions, along with his evaluation of your future prospects with the company. Make certain that you clearly articulate your interest in moving up; also inquire directly if going to a four-day week took you out of contention for the promotion. If this was indeed the case, you have a more serious problem. But raise the question of whether the policy needs review and start building support for a change.

Q: The women in my company throw around a couple of terms that I'm not quite sure I fully understand. What exactly is the "mommy track"? And how about the "glass ceiling"?

A: The mommy track is a slower career track for mothers, allowing them to proceed up the ladder at a slower pace in exchange for a lighter schedule. The glass ceiling refers to an invisible barrier to upward career mobility that women executives may encounter. Take a look at your organizational chart and observe at what level the ranks of women thin out, then note where they disappear altogether. You can probably place your organization's glass ceiling right about there!

ACTION STEPS THAT WORK

1. Talk about inclusive language at a staff meeting of your workgroup. Ask what women want to be called. Pass out a short list with preferred terms.

2. Show the video *The Fairer Sex* to your workgroup and have a discussion of gender bias after looking at the film.

3. Check to be sure that your company has a sexual harassment policy in place and, if it does, reissue it to everyone in your workgroup.

4. Meet with two or three women in your workplace and ask them about the key issues and concerns for women there.

5. Have a meeting with other managers at your level to discuss flexibility in terms of work and family issues. Discuss dilemmas together.

6. Whenever you are hiring a new person for your workgroup, be sure that at least one woman is on the short list of candidates.

CREATING COMPETITIVE ADVANTAGE

Do's	Don'ts
• Do provide women with opportunities to serve on task forces and interact with senior managers. • Do provide training in preventing sexual harassment. • Do make sure your own language is not offensive or sexist. Ask the women in your workgroup to help you with this. • Do find out whether your work environment is supportive to women. Ask the women. Do a survey. Check it out.	• Don't make any assumptions about what kind of job any particular woman may want. • Don't sweep complaints about sexual harassment under the table. Take them seriously. • Don't ignore comments that may be offensive to women; deal with them. Let the speaker know that you find them inappropriate. • Don't rely on who you know and the old-boy network when you are hiring.

RESOURCES

ORGANIZATIONS

Ms. Foundation, 141 Fifth Avenue, Suite 6S, New York, NY 10010.

National Commission on Working Women, Wider Opportunities for Women (WOW), 1325 G Street, NW, Washington, DC 20005; (202) 737-5764.

9 to 5, National Association of Working Women, 614 Superior Avenue, NW, Cleveland, OH 44113-1387; hotline: 1-800-522-0925 (in Cleveland, 621-9449).

Women's Bureau, Office of the Secretary, U.S. Department of Labor, Washington, DC, 20210.

BOOKS

Val Dumond, *The Elements of Nonsexist Usage: A Guide to Inclusive Spoken and Written English*, New York: Prentice-Hall, 1990.

George Simons and Deborah Weissman, *Men and Women: Partners at Work*, Los Altos, CA: Crisp Publications, 1990.

Deborah Tannen, *You Just Don't Understand: Women and Men in Conversation*, New York: William Morris and Company, 1990.

Lynn Martin, Secretary, *A Report on the Glass Ceiling*, U.S. Department of Labor, 1991.

Women's Yellow Pages [New York Pages published by St. Martin's Press, Inc., 175 Fifth Avenue, New York, NY 10010; (212) 674-5151].

ARTICLES

Kathleen Reardon, "The Memo Every Woman Keeps on Her Desk," *Harvard Business Review*, March–April 1993, Report #93209, pp. 4–8.

Judy B. Rosener, "Ways Women Lead," *Harvard Business Review*, November–December 1990, Report #90608, pp. 119–125.

Felice N. Schwartz, "Women as a Business Imperative," *Harvard Business Review*, March–April, 1992, Report #92207, pp. 105–113.

AUDIOVISUALS

Subtle Sexual Harassment, Quality Media Resources; P.O. Box 1706, Bellevue, WA; (800) 800-5129.

The Tale of O, On Being Different in an Organization, Goodmeasure, Cambridge, MA; (617) 621-3838.

The Fairer Sex, CorVision Media, 1359 Barclay Blvd., Buffalo Grove, IL, (800) 537-3130.

The Power of Diversity: Module I: Sexual Harassment and Gender Discrimination, and *Module VI, Balance of Work/Family Issues,* CorVision Media, 1359 Barclay Blvd., Buffalo Grove, IL 60089; (800) 537-3130.

CHAPTER 3

PEOPLE OF COLOR—RACE

THE SUBJECT

AT a conference on the topic of diversity, people were asked to break up into two groups: whites and people of color. Our colleague Marya Muñoz, who is from Puerto Rico, reported her personal confusion. Which group did she belong in? Marya has white, white skin, far whiter than that of 99 percent of those who were going to the white group, strawberry blonde hair, and green eyes. She comes from an old Puerto Rican family of Spanish ancestry, however, and considers herself Hispanic. Finally she decided to join the people of color, but her dilemma suggests some problems with this term.

In this chapter we discuss workplace issues involving people of color. People of color represent 15.5 percent of all employees, 6 percent of all managers, and 2.6 percent of all executives. Before going any further, we need to stop and define some terms. Exactly who, you may be asking, are people of color? And what exactly is race anyway?

The answers to these apparently straightforward questions are complicated. *People of color* is a term designating nonwhites that has gained acceptance in the 1990s. It is one of the terms used to replace minorities. As it becomes clearer that *"minorities"* actually make up the majority of the world, that term has come to seem inappropriate. In addition, *minorities* sounds insulting, ghettoizing, and minimalizing to some. We use the word *Hispanic* here, but we recognize that growing numbers of people prefer *Latino* and *Latina. Chicano,* a term for Mexican-Americans, is the choice of still others.

The term *people of color,* however, is not without its own problems. Many people just don't like it. Some feel it's just a new way of saying "colored." In countries outside the United States, it is frequently misunderstood and heard as derogatory. Frankly, we are using people of color in this chapter because we don't have a better term.

Now, back to race. *What is race?* Traditionally, it was believed that there were three major races, each with its own blood type and physical characteristics. That view has been discredited. Today it is not that simple. The Census Bureau uses four official racial categories: American Indian or Alaskan Native, Asian or Pacific Islander, black, and white. (See Figure 3.1.) Hispanics, who make up roughly 9 percent of the population, can be of any race. (See Figure 3.2.) Hispanic origin is seen as an ethnic category separate from race. During the last decade, the growth rates of blacks, Native Americans, Asians, and Hispanics have been significantly higher than the growth rate of whites. (See Figure 3.3.)

"...How much race matters in the American present...For me, it is an urgent question of power and morality; for others it is an every day matter of life and death."
—CORNEL WEST, *RACE MATTERS*, P. XI

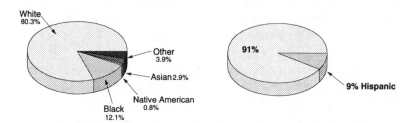

Fig. 3.1 U.S. Population by Race: 1990
Source: U.S. Bureau of the Census.

Fig. 3.2 People of Hispanic Origin: 1990
Source: U.S. Bureau of the Census.

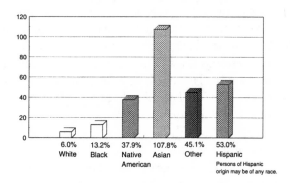

Fig. 3.3 Percentage Growth in Population by Race Between 1980 and 1990
Source: U.S. Bureau of the Census.

In the 1990 census, people who didn't fit one of these four categories were asked to check "Other." Over 9 million, or about one person in twenty-five, checked this response a 45 percent increase since 1980. Many of these "others" are Hispanic and clearly do not see themselves as either black or white. Also, it has been estimated that between 75 percent and 90 percent of the people in the United States classified as black could be multiracial. The number of black and white interracial married couples has increased 78 percent since 1980. Others are a mix of three or more races. Jim Spencer, for example, a diversity consultant at Ibis, is part African-American, part Native American, and part white. There are also new immigrants. As a congressman from Ohio put it, "A deluge of new Americans from every part of the world is overwhelming our traditional racial distinctions."

The Census Bureau is considering adding new categories to the new census, such as "multiracial" and "Middle Easterner." But the problems with racial classifications are numerous, and the distinctions remain confused and arbitrary. Many important workplace decisions, however, such as contracts with the government and grants, are influenced by statistics on the racial background of employees. Race will therefore remain a very important topic in the foreseeable future.

ETHNICITY

In contrast to race, groups with similar culture, customs, and language, but not necessarily biological or physical characteristics, are called ethnic groups. Italians, Jews, Kurds, Slavs, and Latvians are examples of such groups. Hispanics are also an ethnic group, although many people are not aware of this and think of them as a race.

WHAT IS RACISM?

And now for another question. What is racism? Racism is a belief that one race is inherently superior to others. A continuum of prejudice exists in this country. The darker the skin tone, the more disdain, prejudice, and discrimination a typical person faces. Whites continue to hold the vast majority of the positions of power in our corporations and government agencies, as well as most positions of power in our educational, health-care, and religious institutions.

"Can you imagine if this country were not so afflicted with racism? Can you imagine what it would be like if the vitality, humor, and resilience of the black American were infused throughout this country?"
—MAYA ANGELOU, IN BRIAN LANKER, *I DREAM A WORLD,* 1989

Despite the fact that most people believe that they, as individuals, are fair, people of color, for the most part, are not part of the senior management in organizations in this country. Almost all people of color feel that the system doesn't work fairly for them as a group, although it is certainly true that more than a few individuals have succeeded. Racist attitudes seem to be the most difficult of all attitudes to alter. To this day, it is evident that people of color, on the whole, have not achieved positions of power in proportion to their numbers in the population.

A recent study indicated that slightly more than half of the Americans in the workforce prefer to work with people of their own race. Those employees with more experience actually working with people of other races, however, show a stronger preference for diversity than others. In fact, the study goes on to say, work is the primary place where people from different races meet and can get to know one another. Most people live in communities that are quite segregated; they pray in temples, mosques, and churches that are segregated and most attended segregated schools.

THE LAW

The Civil Rights Act of 1866 was one of the earliest attempts to protect people of color against discrimination on the basis of race. The Civil Rights Act of 1964 (Title VII) prohibits discrimination in employment on the basis of race, color, sex, religion, or national origin. This is the law that forms the basis for equal employment opportunity (EEO) and most charges of discrimination, at least on the federal level. Most states have similar antidiscrimination laws.

Title VII of the 1964 act makes it unlawful for employers to discriminate on the basis of race or color. Such prohibition extends to a racially hostile work environment, and this means that the workplace must be free of racial insults and intimidation. In addition, race or color can virtually never be a bona fide occupational qualification. The Equal Employment Opportunity Commission (EEOC) issues guidelines to help employers understand the letter and spirit of the Civil Rights Act.

The Civil Rights Act of 1991 provides employees charging intentional discrimination the right to a jury trial and the right to recover punitive and compensatory damages. This provides individual employees with more protection than before. Executive Order 11242 requires employers who hold federal contracts or subcontracts of $50,000 or more and have fifty or more employees to prepare written affirmative action plans to ensure increases in the hiring, training, and promotion of people of color (and women) into jobs and levels where they are seriously underrepresented.

Employers are required to set goals to correct "conspicuous imbalance" when there is a large difference between the percentage of people of color employed and the percentage of qualified people of color in the area.

The degree to which companies comply with this law varies. Reports must be filed with the government, however, and these reports are audited from time to time. Several major corporations have been heavily fined for noncompliance, which is part of the reason companies today strive to be sure they meet the letter of the law. Many employers take affirmative action steps even though they are not required to. They have decided it is simply good for business.

COMMON ISSUES AND CONCERNS

Four major issues involving people of color emerge from our interviews of thousands of people in the workplace, including hundreds of people of color.

UNDERREPRESENTATION OF PEOPLE OF COLOR

There are few people of color at the top and middle levels of the organizational pyramid. But perhaps even more startling is the absence of people of color at any level in the typical American workplace. (See Figure 3.4.) There is almost always a significantly smaller percentage of people of color in the workplace than in the general geographic location. Managers and supervisors typically tell us that they would like to hire more people of color. "The problem is that there just aren't any qualified candidates," they tell us. "We have tried very hard, but Human Resources just doesn't put minority candidates in front of us."

"Although many forms of exclusion and discrimination exist in this country, none is so deeply rooted, persistent, and intractable as that based on color."
—J. HOPPS

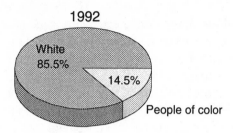

1992

White
85.5%

14.5%

People of color

Fig. 3.4 People of Color in the Labor Force
Source: U.S. Bureau of Labor Statistics.

OUR COMMENT

We can't buy this. It seems like the rationale of the half-hearted. In most organizations, we observe that little effort has actually been made to find candidates of color. Many managers and supervisors continue to rely on word of mouth for hiring and use the same old sources to locate candidates. This all but ensures that the status quo will be maintained, as finding candidates of color usually takes a concerted effort. Recruiting at an expanded list of colleges, advertising in some local minority newspapers, or selecting a recruiter who specializes in minority hiring are the kinds of actions that have been found effective.

PERSISTING STEREOTYPES

When we interview blacks, Latinos, Native Americans, and Asian-Americans in organizations across the country, the vast majority report that the people of color in their organization face widely accepted stereotypes. Stereotypes, as we define them, are rigid, over-simplified, and often distorted generalizations about a group. For example, at one large corporation in 1994, the company president was meeting with a black middle manager. The president made two comments to the manager, one about the most recent basketball tournament and another about the O.J. Simpson murder trial. The manager was gracious, but he told us he felt stereotyped by these comments which assumed his interests were primarily on topics relating to his being black. Even more hurtful are stereotypes about being less reliable, less intelligent, and less competent. People of color react to being stereotyped in a number of different ways. Some become frustrated, angry, or bitter. Others feel depressed and hopeless and stop trying to get ahead. White people are often unaware of the intensity of these kinds of feelings on the part of people of color.

> "...We have all been programmed to respond to the human differences between us with fear and loathing and to handle that difference in one of three ways: ignore it, and if that is not possible, copy it if we think it is dominant, or destroy it if we think it is subordinate. But we have no patterns for relating across our human differences as equal."
> —AUDRE LOURDE, *SISTER OUTSIDER*

Asian-Americans, often labeled the "successful minority," share many of these same feelings, although they may tend to be even less outspoken. In general, their most common complaint revolves around not being fairly recognized for their achievements and, at times, they feel that they are being criticized for working too hard. Many report that it is much harder for them to earn a promotion than for others.

OUR COMMENT
First, most people have trouble recognizing their stereotypes for what they are and even more difficulty in seeing specific individuals apart from their group identity. Whites typically have the additional blinders of not even thinking of themselves as white and being completely out of touch with the advantages that their whiteness brings them. The majority of white managers still do not understand the nature of institutional racism and how organizational systems can work to exclude people of color. Managers assume that if they are trying to be fair, that's all that matters.

For people of color, on the other hand, racism is an obvious fact of life. Most know for a fact that the system works in both obvious and subtle ways to keep people of color clustered at the bottom of the corporate ladder. (See Figures 3.5 and 3.6.) We think that all employees can benefit from increasing their awareness of racism and stereotyping. It is helpful to grapple with one's own cultural bias and unchallenged assumptions. Training programs and educational events are good ways to further this developmental process.

GETTING STUCK—ROADBLOCKS TO ADVANCEMENT
People of color consistently report that they are promoted much more slowly than their white counterparts and that sooner or later they are

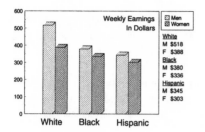

Fig. 3.5 Median Weekly Earnings of Full-Time
Wage and Salary Workers: 1992
Source: U.S. Bureau of Labor Statistics.

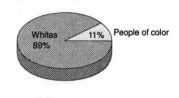

Fig. 3.6 Managerial and Professional
Workers: 1993
Source: U.S. Bureau of Labor Statistics.

blocked by an impervious glass ceiling. Statistical studies of individual organizations back this up. People of color tell us such things as the following: "I have to prove myself over and over again." "There are no higher-level African-Americans, Latinos, or Asians in my organization, so there are no mentors or role models for any of us." "Getting ahead in this organization depends on who you know." "Native Americans are never seen in the senior most ranks of my organization."

OUR COMMENT

It is true that getting ahead in today's workplace often does depend upon who you know. In practice, in most organizations, visibility and access to more senior people are as important as competence and performance. And people of color are seldom part of the old-boy network that is calling the shots and identifying the rising stars. They don't usually play golf with the senior managers, they may not live in the same town with them, they don't go to the same parties, and they don't belong to the same clubs. It is through these social interactions that friendships develop and, most critically, where important information about jobs is exchanged.

People want to hire or promote the very best person available. They tend to select people they know, however. They believe that it is just coincidental that they choose people who look like them, were educated like them, and share a similar lifestyle. They tell us obliquely that it is too risky to promote people of color, who may have a different style, a different way of thinking. Those that hire seek someone predictable, someone who will think as they do. So they hire people of color as affirmative action officers, for human resources, as secretaries, as maintenance workers, or for the shipping department.

Though the overall picture is discouraging, a number of companies have made enormous investments in helping to further the careers of people of color. The Bank of America in Los Angeles has made extensive use of career strategy seminars for Asian-American, Hispanic, and African-American officers of the bank. All 65,000 US WEST managers and employees have attended training programs on diversity. The company also offered a program entitled "Accelerated Development Program for Women of Color." These programs are making a difference.

LACK OF ACCOUNTABILITY

When surveyed or asked in interviews, white employees report that some of the people of color in their organization are "getting away with murder." In particular, we hear that Native Americans and African-Americans can scoff at the rules and nothing happens. They come in early, leave late, and produce far less than others. Their coworkers explain that supervisors don't dare hold people of color accountable because they are so afraid of the company being sued.

OUR COMMENT

It is interesting to note that people of color usually believe that they are held to a much higher standard of behavior than their white counterparts, while many whites see the situation as just the opposite— they see people of color as protected, spared the harsh realities of today's competitive work climate. It is true that some supervisors and managers are afraid to give people of color negative feedback. But, far from being an advantage for people of color, this is really a significant handicap for them. They are not given the opportunity to learn about their mistakes or about which aspects of their job performance need improving.

We suggest that you review the kind of feedback that the people of color in your workgroup receive. This means looking at both the formal performance appraisal process and more informal coaching practices. Be sure that there are good systems in place and that they are being properly implemented. Many managers and supervisors don't give anyone negative feedback. It matters less to white people, because they usually have more access to mentors and friends who will give them the inside story.

WORKING EXAMPLES
"CAN'T YOU TAKE A JOKE?"

Mazelle, a black woman working in a Florida factory, tells us about the kidding that she and her black coworkers get from the white majority. For example, her supervisor teasingly calls her "Aunt Jemima." A new black supervisor in her workplace found a watermelon on his desk his first day on the job. He was extremely upset. A Native American in Colorado was hurt when he was given a bow and arrow as a joke birthday present by his workgroup. An Asian woman was offended when a woman in her workgroup kept kidding about a Chinese fire drill.

> "All this comes out of the experience of racism I share with other Asian-Americans or other people of color, and this experience is not merely one of insults or prejudices but also entails a search for a place where I feel safe to own and express my own experience."
> —DAVID MURA

OUR COMMENT

It is up to you as the supervisor or manager to stop this kind of humor. People of color often feel afraid to speak up and complain because they fear they will be seen as poor sports. Whenever you hear about these kinds of jokes, you need to act. Make it very clear to everyone in your workgroup that racially based humor or comments are unacceptable in today's workplace. Ask people to tell you if they are offended.

And, of course, as a manager or supervisor, you have to set the tone for the rest of the group. Awareness of what is appropriate and what is not varies widely. It is up to you to be more sensitive than anyone else and to educate the group, since much of this humor is not intended as a put-down. Ask for some management training for yourself and any people of color who are managers in your organization. At Apple Computer, for example, each manager is given a guide that outlines good management behavior from a multicultural perspective.

BACKLASH

Two white employees, Frank Bertrand and Steve Fletcher, tell you that they are upset because José Vizcaino, who is Puerto Rican, got promoted into the technician's job in their workgroup. José reports that everyone assumes he got the job just because of EEO, not because he deserved it. His coworkers told him, "They are just using you to fill a quota—You'd never get this job otherwise." José feels it is hopeless to try to convince anyone that he's well qualified. You observe that he is ignored by the other technicians and that he is always alone.

OUR COMMENT

This is a serious problem. José is in jeopardy. With no support from his coworkers, his performance may drop. Consider intervening in several ways. First, tell Steve, Frank, and all the others in the workgroup exactly why you promoted José. If it is not an EEO appointment, tell them that. If diversity was a factor, explain to them why diversity is important for the business. Let them know that you expect them to welcome José and give him the same kind of informal on-the-job training that they'd give anyone else. Stay in touch with José over the next weeks to see how the situation evolves.

QUESTIONS AND ANSWERS

Q: When I hear the guys in my group using words like "nigger," I panic. I know that this is a bad word, but what can I actually say to them that won't sound stupid?

A: It is difficult to stop this kind of racial slur, but here are a few all-purpose comments to have ready the next time you hear one of these affronts: "That word bothers me," or "I find that word offensive." For your direct reports, you need to say something stronger like, "That kind of language is not acceptable, and I don't want to hear it again in this workgroup."

Q: An African-American woman in my workgroup named Sallie James comes to work late almost every day. I have heard that being late is typical of blacks. Should I accept this as a cultural difference?

A: Whether this is a cultural difference or not in debatable. In any case, if you need people there on time, of course work with Sallie about the issue. Valuing differences does not mean lowering standards or sacrificing quality. You need to talk to Sallie about the reasons for lateness in her particular case—it may well be that there are family problems or some other difficulty that you can help with. But if it interferes with the work getting done, it must be dealt with.

Q: I work at a high-tech company that has very few people of color. Because I'm Latino, I think, I get appointed to every task force or committee in the company. Then I get asked, "What do Hispanics think about this or that? I'm annoyed. How can I stop this?"

A: It can get burdensome. I'd urge you to tactfully let people know when you feel that they are overworking you. Even more important, let people know that you can't speak for all Latinos. Say that all you can do is speak for yourself. How about suggesting that they hire a few more people of color and even, perhaps, that you will help them?

Q: My company recently began a "valuing differences" program, and one of its first events was a series of panel discussions featuring members of different minority groups. I'm a Japanese-American. I was asked to sit on a panel with coworkers who are Korean, Chinese, and Cambodian. I'm irritated that such a program didn't respect *our* differences but assumed that we're all one and the same—kind of interchangeable Asian-Americans. Some of my colleagues say I'm being too fussy.

A: Americans *do* tend to lump people together; we tend to not make distinctions. However, many groups within our country identify extremely closely with their specific roots. Anything you can do to educate your fellow workers about intergroup differences would be a good contribution to their evolving state of awareness. But don't be oversensitive, it sounds as if your company has good intentions.

Q: I'm a fifty-four-year-old white female who is a unit coordinator in a major teaching hospital. A group of us went out for lunch recently, and one of my colleagues (who happens to be a black male) commented bitterly about some racist graffiti in the men's room. He claimed that he'd reported their appearance over six weeks ago, and yet they were still present. The rest rooms get used by a lot of people—the general public as well as staff and outpatients. These things happen throughout society—does he really have a gripe?

A: Yes! We think failure to remove the racist graffiti in the rest room promptly implies something about the hospital; this could range from a sense that the institution doesn't feel that dealing with racism is a priority to an implication that the institution actually condones racism. The bottom line here is these graffiti offend everyone who uses the facility. They must be removed immediately, for the benefit of both lavatory users and the hospital itself. Report them yourself.

Q: Our radio station softball team has named itself the Redskins because this word uses our call letters. Nonetheless, one of our interns has objected, saying that we're being insensitive to Native Americans. Do we need to change our name?

A: We think you should consider it. Native Americans have told us that they resent being presented as mascots. The important question is always whether the station is taking action to tackle the truly major issues of diversity. That is where attention and resources should be directed. However, there is no need to offend people, and while this may seem like a frivolous quibble to you, it is a serious issue for others.

Q: I'm a white male supervisor in a film processing facility that runs twenty-four hours a day. No matter what shift is on, however, the pattern in the cafeteria at mealtimes is always the same: The black workers sit together at one table. This makes me somewhat uncomfortable when I come out of the food line with my tray—I'm torn between sitting with my friends and a desire to support minority employees. Should I go over and sit at the black table sometimes?

A: This is a delicate issue. Your intentions sound good, but they may be problematic. Do you have friends among the blacks who are seated together? Generally, people seek comfortable, relaxed situations during their breaks; that is why like sorts of people often sit together. If you have friends at the black table, you may be welcome there; we'd suggest you raise the issue with your friends prior to plopping down, however. Most importantly, you have expressed a desire to support a multicultural workforce in your organization, and there are many other ways to show support.

Q: I'd be open to hiring nonwhite candidates, but Human Resources never sends me any. What should I do?

A: Your organization needs to be alerted to the fact that it can no longer take a passive role in bringing on new employees if it wishes to diversify its workforce. Make an appointment with Human Resources and express your views. Ask how the department goes about informing the public about job openings, and explain your concern about the stream of all white candidates you have been sent in response to your requisitions. Say that you believe that it is critical that the pool be expanded, and offer to assist in making sure this happens.

Q: Our staff meetings are brutal. People are rude and cut each other off. Whenever one of the two black women in our meeting speaks up, the rest of the group seems to ignore her remarks. The conversation continues as if nothing had been contributed, and then, to add insult to injury, later on someone else offers the same idea and gets credit for it! I'm sick of it! What do you suggest?

A: Our suggestion would be to tackle the entire issue of revamping your meetings. First of all, in the circus you describe, it is unlikely you will be able to successfully initiate a different pattern of response to the two employees about whom you are concerned. Consider having a meeting to talk about meetings! Perhaps show the film "Meetings, Bloody Meetings."[1] Then establish some new ground rules to ensure order and respect. If necessary, you may have to underscore the contributions of the two black women for a while to make sure that they get heard.

ACTION STEPS THAT WORK

1. Sit down with anyone in your workgroup who is of a different racial background and ask them, "What is it like for people of color to work here?" You may be amazed at what you learn. If you are a person of color yourself, tell people about your own experiences.

[1] *Meetings Bloody Meetings* (Video), Video Arts, Inc., 8614 West Catalpa Ave., Chicago, IL 60656, Revised 1994.

2. Start a buddy or mentoring system for new employees who are interested, with higher-level mentors. Encourage people of color to get a mentor, as it will instantly create communication across racial lines.
3. Encourage your organization to support black, Latino, Asian-American, or other support/networking groups within the workplace. Xerox made real progress in achieving racial balance through its black caucus. There's a video on this that points the way.
4. Give out articles to your workgroup that will start educating them about diversity and racism. We recommend Roosevelt Thomas's article "From Affirmative Action to Valuing Diversity." Show them the video *True Colors*.
5. Ask your company to provide training on diversity and racism for your workgroup.

CREATING COMPETITIVE ADVANTAGE

Do's	Don'ts
• Do discuss this book with several managers in your organization.	• Don't ignore racial slurs. Speak up about their inappropriateness.
• Do tell your workgroup what you see as the business reasons for more diversity.	• Don't omit negative feedback on job performance to people of color.
• Do widen your pool of candidates for all jobs and promotions.	• Don't ask a person of color to speak for all African-Americans, Latinos, etc.
• Do ask the people of color in your workgroup about the work environment.	• Don't assume that people of color who don't speak up have no issues.
• Do hold career conversations with people of color in your workgroup.	• Don't assume that because individuals are trying to be fair, the system is fair.

RESOURCES

ORGANIZATIONS

The Institute for Managing Diversity, Inc., 830 Westview Drive S.W., Atlanta, GA 30314; (404) 524-7316.

NAACP (National Association for the Advancement of Colored People), 4805 Mount Hope Drive, Baltimore, MD 21215; (410) 358-8900.

BOOKS

Lawrence Otis Graham, *The Best Companies for Minorities*, New York: A Plume Book, 1993.

Janet E. Helms, *A Race is a Nice Thing to Have: A Guide to Being a White Person or Understanding the White Person in Your Life*, Topeka, KS: Content Communications, 1992.

Steps to Resolving Racial Conflict at the Workplace, Ontario Federation of Labor, 15 Gervais Drive, Suite 202, Don Mills, Ontario, Canada, M3C148. A how-to guide for shop standards and union personnel.

Barb Thomas and Charles Norogrodsky, *Combating Racism in the Workplace: A Course for Workers*, Cross Cultural Communications Centre, 965 Bloor St., West Toronto, Ontario, Canada M6H1R7.

Cornel West, *Race Matters*, Boston: Beacon Press, 1993.

ARTICLES

Peggy McIntosh, *White Privilege and Male Privilege*, Working Papers #189, Wellesley College Center for Research, Wellesley, MA, 1988.

Roosevelt Thomas, "From Affirmative Action to Valuing Diversity," *Harvard Business Review*, March–April 1990, pp. 107–117.

"25 Best Places for Blacks to Work," *Black Enterprise*, February 1992, pp. 71–96.

"1992 Hispanic 100: The One Hundred Companies Providing the Most Opportunities for Hispanics," *Hispanic*, January–February 1992, pp. 49–76.

AUDIOVISUALS

Black Caucus at Xerox, MacNeil Lehrer News Hour, Oct. 29, 1991, A PBS Video Production, 1320 Braddock Place, Alexandria, VA 22314-1698; 1-800-344-3337. For a transcript call Journal Graphics, 303-831-9000.

True Colors, BBP, 24 Rope Ferry Road, Waterford, CT 06386; (800) 243-0876

The Power of Diversity, Module III Career Development: Minority Issues, CorVision Media, 1359 Barclay Blvd., Buffalo Grove, IL 60089; (800) 537-3130.

CHAPTER 4

OLDER EMPLOYEES—AGE

THE SUBJECT

"ALL the older people in my group are joked about," says a young employee in a high-tech company. "With all the technological changes, it's hard for older workers to keep up; they are really slow at picking up things," says another.

It's tough to be an older worker in today's workplace. Americans used to say that "life begins at forty." No longer. Today older people are often considered obsolete, expendable, and disposable. People over forty often feel in peril, worrying constantly whether they are going to get the axe. According to a University of Pennsylvania study reported in the *Wall Street Journal* on June 13, 1994, "Some 25 percent of workers aged fifty-one to sixty-one feel they have a 50/50 chance of being laid off without benefits within a year."

Who then, in the workplace, is considered old? It's hard to say, because there are so many different definitions of "old" floating around. The federal government is inconsistent. The chief law barring discrimination by age takes forty as its starting point. The Department of Labor sometimes uses age forty-five, and at other times fifty-five. The Administration on Aging takes age sixty as its benchmark, while Social Security has enshrined age sixty-five (and also sixty-two).

Because age is a relative concept, we prefer not to single out any one birthday as the beginning of older employee status. Much depends on the situation. It even varies from industry to industry. In advertising agencies, for example, people over forty will probably be looked upon as old; in Detroit's auto assembly plants, middle-aged workers became the norm in the middle 1990s as younger employees are relatively few. And it is not unusual for lawyers and some other professionals to practice well into their eighties.

By the year 2000, 13 percent of the population will be over age sixty-five (almost 35 million), as contrasted with only 4.1 percent in

1900. This "graying of America" is one of the major social changes of the twentieth century. At the same time, the numbers of both children and young adults are expected to decrease. Such shifts are bound to affect the workplace dramatically, creating new patterns of work, leisure, and retirement.

"The bottom line is that despite employers' beliefs that older individuals are very good workers, market forces so far have not been strong enough to move most employers to deal with the specific concerns of older workers."
—RICHARD S. BELOUS, ECONOMIST

Definitions of age are also changing radically. As the baby boomers (those born between 1946 and 1964) come to midlife, age fifty and above seems less old than it used to. Improved health and more opportunities make older Americans appear younger than ever before.

Many writers and thinkers are now trying to redefine aging. Betty Friedan, for example, in her book *The Fountain of Age*, rejects the model of later life as a time of decline. Instead, she extols advanced years as an era of personal flowering: "I wonder if age, in fact, may offer the opportunity to develop values and abilities, for each of us and for society, that are not visible or fully realized in youth."[1]

Similarly, the physician Deepak Chopra suggests in his book *Ageless Body, Timeless Mind* that the effects of aging are largely preventable, claiming, for instance, that "awareness has the power to change aging."[2]

Yet these revisions in thinking have not, by and large, taken hold in America's workplaces. There, despite the presence of more than 15 million workers over age fifty-five, the country's infatuation with youth retains its power over corporate decision makers. To be young means to be dynamic; being even middle-aged suggests stodginess, a threat to the image of the company. And to be old is to be vulnerable.

Not surprisingly, therefore, some people will do anything to make themselves look younger. A powerful witness to this fact is the $3 billion spent annually on cosmetic surgery, a fair amount of it by Americans willing to suffer pain in order to reduce signs of aging. On a less drastic note, Friedan refers to a woman of sixty-three who, after

---

[1] Betty Friedan, *The Fountain of Age*, New York: Simon and Schuster, 1993, p. 85.

[2] Deepak Chopra, *Ageless Body, Timeless Mind: The Quantum Alternative to Growing Old*, New York: Harmony Books, 1993, p. 51.

being forced out of her job, dyed her hair and spent $280 on a miniskirt in a vain effort to look young.

Reporters to Gloria Steinem on her 40th birthday: "Gloria, you don't look 40." Steinem's retort: "Gentlemen, this is 40."

Workplace managers tend to have mixed feelings about older employees. In survey after survey, bosses characterize older workers positively in terms of work habits, productivity, and loyalty. Supervisors speak well of older employees' punctuality and reliability. At the same time, managers remain doubtful about the ability of these workers to compete. Are they prepared to learn the new skills necessary to survive in the new conditions of American business? Many of their managers doubt it. Older workers are often seen as plateauing in job development and lacking state-of-the-art skills. People middle-aged and older are considered "over the hill," prone to sickness and absenteeism, and entirely set in their ways.

Some younger managers also feel a generation gap when they are exposed to disapproval and sometimes downright correction by direct reports older than themselves. One forty-year-old bank manager complained in a *Wall Street Journal* interview: "They are like my father telling me what to do."

So a curious situation has developed around older workers: In many places they are respected, valued, and even retained beyond normal retirement age; in other organizations, however, they receive little if any encouragement to develop further and are pressured out of their jobs at the earliest opportunity.

There has been an unrelenting trend toward early retirement in the last decade. In spite of this trend, however, there will be a dramatic increase in the number of older workers in the American workplaces of the future. Projections based on Bureau of Labor Statistics data show that between the years 1995 and 2005, the fastest-growing segment of the workforce will be fifty-five to sixty-four-year-olds, with numbers increasing by 38 percent.

In 1990, 12.3 percent of the workers in the workforce were over fifty-five years old. (See Figure 4.1.) Many experts predict that a shortage of younger workers may require even greater numbers of people over fifty-five to stay in the labor market. In addition, it may be that early retirement will become a luxury that people cannot

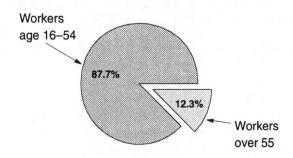

Fig. 4.1 Workers over 55 as a Percentage of the Workforce: 1990
Source: U.S. Bureau of Labor Statistics.

afford. Thus, it is not at all unlikely that in the latter 1990s, individual managers can expect to deal with more older workers than ever before.

THE LAW

Workers over forty are protected by the federal Age Discrimination in Employment Act, which first became law in 1967. A major change for older workers came in 1986, when an amendment to the 1967 law banned compulsory retirement at any age for almost all workers. Another change, in 1991, did away with a two-year statute of limitations on age discrimination lawsuits.

This federal legislation says that age cannot be used to discriminate in any employment decision, including hiring, promotion, firing, wages, and other actions affecting work. A federal agency, the Equal Employment Opportunity Commission (EEOC), has responsibility for enforcing this law across the nation.

In addition, most states have laws prohibiting age discrimination in employment. Frequently they are more restrictive than the federal laws. For example, although the federal law applies only to companies with twenty or more employees, the Commonwealth of Massachusetts extends coverage to workplaces with six or more.

In recent years the number of age discrimination cases has soared. Nationwide, complaints brought to the EEOC totaled more than 30,000 in 1992, and damages amounting to $100 million were assessed. (See Figure 4.2.)

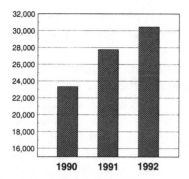

Fig. 4.2 Numbers of Age Discrimination Cases Filed with the EEOC
 Source: Equal Employment Opportunity Commission.

COMMON ISSUES AND CONCERNS
YOU CAN'T TEACH AN OLD DOG NEW TRICKS: LEARNING CAPACITY

Many managers and supervisors stereotype older employees as having major problems learning new technologies or work procedures. For example, older workers are often considered exceptional if they can learn even the rudiments of word processing. From this point of view, job obsolescence is practically unavoidable, and there is little point in offering older employees training opportunities.

OUR COMMENT

Whatever truth the dog proverb may contain, it certainly cannot be applied to older people across the board. It used to be thought that human learning capacity declined sharply after middle age; and scientific research seemed to justify this view. But that idea has been largely discredited by more up-to-date research. Studies have shown that most older people can acquire new knowledge and new skills. The only difference is that their rate of learning may be somewhat slower. What seems to be critical for ongoing learning is keeping the brain exercised and stimulated.

Of course, some individual veteran employees are poor learners. They may be like Bob, an unemployed West Coast high tech manager, who, according to the business pages of the *New York Times*, blames himself for not having kept up. He says, "I thought I could leave the intense technology skills to the college graduates and I would be their leader." He thought that "being a people person, not a tech person, would be enough. In hindsight, that was a big mistake."[3]

FISH OUT OF WATER: ADAPTING TO CHANGE
Some older employees find themselves out of synch with the contemporary workplace culture. They look back to the "good old days" when the organization was more of a family. The "lean and mean" approach of many companies puts them off and makes them feel nervous. They feel out of place in conversations when their younger coworkers talk about the likes of Michael Jackson, Madonna, Seinfeld, or MTV. Newfangled work arrangements such as virtual teams, job sharing, and teleconferencing mystify them.

OUR COMMENT
It makes sense that many older workers feel overwhelmed by change; many younger workers feel the same way. More workplace changes have occurred in the last ten years than in the previous thirty. In particular, the psychological contract—the unwritten understanding between employees and their organizations about job security—has been broken in most organizations. It is no longer true that if employees perform their jobs well, the organization will take care of them. That can be bewildering.

Despite these facts, however, we caution against sweeping generalizations and stereotypes concerning older workers. What you must do as a manager or supervisor is look at older people on a case-by-case basis. Yes, some older employees are unteachable. Many are not. The question is not, "How old is this worker?" but, "How well is this person doing the job?" And, most importantly, "What can I do to help him or her continue to contribute to the organization?"

NOT CUTTING THE MUSTARD: PERFORMANCE PROBLEMS
Often performance problems in an older worker build up very slowly over months and years. What may have been an occasional lapse five years ago becomes more of a pattern over time. In our focus groups, most complaints we hear about older workers are related to using computers, accepting new procedures, and clinging to old ways of

[3] Michelle Quinn, New York Times, Jan. 23, 1994, Sec. F, p. 5.

working. But we hear the same kind of complaints about all workers. Only when it's an older person is the person labeled a dinosaur.

OUR COMMENT

When older employees do have performance problems, taking action can be difficult. Often managers avoid discussing the problems altogether. Why? First, because they don't want to hurt anybody's feelings. Second, managers often feel protective about an older person. And, third, many of us have been taught not to criticize our elders. All these reasons may be in play, plus the usual one that managers often don't give any workers negative feedback.

UNSPLENDID ISOLATION

If you have only a few older employees, problems can arise from that fact. The thinner their ranks, the more difficult the experience of the workplace may be for them. We know a very successful toy salesman in New Jersey who loved his job. At age sixty-six, however, he got more and more depressed because all his pals had left the company. As he put it, "There's no one to talk to." He said to his wife, "It just isn't fun any more."

> "The human race is faced with a cruel choice: work or daytime television."
> —UNKNOWN

OUR COMMENT

There is bias against hiring older people. Many of those over fifty struggle to land a job. We think of the unemployed engineer, a 1959 graduate of Harvard College, who reported sending out ten thousand résumés and getting absolutely no responses! It is hard to believe that this man did not merit a second look by anyone.

We suggest that you take a new look at your own hiring practices. Do you hire only people just out of school? Do you throw out résumés if the person is over forty-five? Do you require such specific qualifications that no one who graduated twenty years ago can ever be considered? This limits your chances for age diversity, a mix of coins just minted along with those that have been in circulation for a while. In some companies, promotions are rarely, if ever, offered to people over fifty-five. The reasons given are that not promoting older workers will save money and is a way to retain the organization's rising stars.

"Expanding employment opportunities [for older workers] is a win, win situation."
—PETER LIBASSI, SENIOR VICE PRESIDENT, THE TRAVELERS COMPANIES, 1990

Consider doing an informal audit of age groups in your work area. The Grumman Corporation and other progressive companies have instituted audits to determine whether they have a reasonable spread of ages in their workplaces. They feel that a balanced workforce is desirable, as it helps with succession planning. The audit helps them identify age groups in which there are few employees.

When it does come time for downsizing, older workers typically are the first to go. Don't fall into this trap; look at each worker on a case-by-case basis. Also, take note of the unarticulated, yet often enormous, organizational knowledge that some older workers possess. And, of course, if older workers are eliminated in far greater proportion than others, you may be leaving your organization open to a lawsuit.

WORKING EXAMPLES
DEPRESSED, BUT HANGING ON

George Roberts works as an engineer in an international corporation that specializes in photographic products. On his next birthday he will be sixty-four years old. George used to enjoy his work and frequently called himself a "company man." But those days are long gone. He now feels stalemated, stuck in a position without much hope of more money or a new challenge. Most of his satisfaction these days comes from the small-scale engineering projects he tinkers with at home.

He has noticed that younger employees, formerly at his level, have been given opportunities for retraining and have gone on to better-paying jobs with more authority. George also fears that his skills are lagging behind the changing workplace. Not knowing how to use the latest computerized design programs, for example, has put him at a definite disadvantage.

"The bottom line is that despite employers' beliefs that older individuals are very good workers, market forces so far have not been strong enough to move most employers to deal with the specific concerns of older workers."
—RICHARD S. BELOUS, ECONOMIST

Our Comment

George finds himself in a work environment that is ignoring his needs. But this is not rare: Studies show that only 30 percent of American employers provide training for their older employees. As George's satisfaction on the job has diminished, he has turned his best energies to interests outside of his job—a loss for the company!

Three approaches could help. First, the situation cries out for communication. George's manager needs to sit down and talk to him about his wants and needs. Get the issues on the table. Second, George and his manager should explore together alternatives like restructuring the job description and retraining. Finally, it might help both George and the company to talk about a bridge job or a phase-out schedule. Eventual retirement is a fact of life, and a gradual phasing down can often be best for all parties. This process might involve more flexible work arrangements, such as part-time work, job sharing, or home-based work. (See Figure 4.3.)

Caught in the Downsizing Crunch

Molly Greenberg works as a supervisor in a leading temporary help agency. At fifty-six, she is the oldest member of the permanent staff. She feels her experience to be an asset in helping her do a good job. The other staff members seem to value Molly's maturity. They sometimes take her aside and ask her advice about job problems or even issues in their private lives.

Her tenure in this position has resulted in Molly's pay per hour being far greater than that of anyone else in the office. Because of that fact, she worries about her job security. The company is not doing

Stages in Career Development	Issues	Specific Tasks
Late career in nonleadership role	Becoming a mentor Broadening interests Deepening skills	Remaining technically competent Developing interpersonal skills Dealing with younger persons
Late career in leadership role	Using skills and talents for organization's welfare Selecting and developing subordinates	Becoming more responsible for organization Handling power Balancing career and family
Decline and disengagement	Learning to accept reduced power and responsibility	Finding new sources of satisfaction
Retirement	Adjusting to more drastic lifestyle changes	Maintaining a sense of identity and self-worth without job

Fig. 4.3 Career Stages and Issues for Older Employees
Source: *Career Dynamics: Matching Individual and Organizational Needs,* E.H. Schein, 1978

well financially, and a new young boss has been transferred in. Molly suspects that a younger woman is being groomed to take over her job.

OUR COMMENT

Most companies that give annual raises will encounter situations such as Molly's. Succinctly put, Molly is making a great deal more than other people who are doing comparable work. The question that is uppermost in the employer's mind is, Is she worth it?

In reality, it may not matter because it is illegal to terminate Molly simply to replace her with a less experienced, younger employee. Some companies deal with this situation by creating a salary review system that caps the upper end of the pay range for a specific function. Other firms, as part of the severance package, require workers to sign a release saying that they will not sue the company. The Older Workers Benefit Protection Act imposes extra requirements if such a release is to be valid for an older worker. These may or may not hold up in a court of law.

The best approach is to play it straight. It is simply against the law for companies to single out employees for termination on the basis of age. If they are not doing the job, of course, it is a different matter. Deal with older workers as individuals, case by case. People vary enormously in the length of time they can work productively and efficiently. Beware of stereotypes and of dealing with older people as a monolithic group.

STUCK IN THE PAST: FAILURE TO CHANGE

A large defense contractor with a reputation for never laying anyone off fired a group of about a dozen employees who failed to adapt to the times. They were experts in a technology that for decades had been in great demand. As a result, they had flourished for many years as their company continued to receive contracts from the Pentagon for products that depended on their engineering skills.

The time came, however, a few years ago, when this technology was outdated. When top managers recognized that the skills of these veteran employees were no longer usable, the well-meaning company offered them many opportunities for training in new and needed technologies. However, every single one of them said no to these opportunities. In time, the company felt forced to take drastic action, and, to the regret of everyone concerned, all of these long-time employees lost their jobs.

OUR COMMENT

The reasons why these older employees refused opportunities to change are not altogether clear, but some partial explanations have emerged. For one thing, the company had a long history of relaxed work conditions and little emphasis on ongoing professional development. Having a sure-fire source of contracts meant that the corporation did not need to be lean and mean. In this atmosphere, employees did not feel much need to prepare for radical change.

Second, this particular group of employees had a large psychological investment in their specific skills. As the company manager whom we interviewed said, "These guys had made their reputations in this engineering field and were in widespread demand. They used to go around the country speaking on their subject and as a result enjoyed much prestige."

Members of this group were unable to change their work habits and mindsets of many years standing. How could they have been salvaged? The point of this story is that sometimes, no matter how hard you try, you can fail with certain employees.

QUESTIONS AND ANSWERS

Q: Don't older people get sick much more often than younger men and women? Isn't their rate of absenteeism on the job higher than others', and isn't their health insurance more expensive?

A: Actually, people between the ages of fifty and seventy-five get sick less often than those in their twenties and thirties. True, people over fifty have more chronic illnesses than their juniors, but such ailments usually do not interfere with work. Data indicate that the absentee rate for employees who are middle-aged and older is at least as good as that for younger workers. Surveys of human resources executives done by the Daniel Yankelovich Group also give high marks to older employees for attendance and punctuality. Over 90 percent of employers rated these employees excellent or very good. You are right that health insurance usually does cost somewhat more for older workers, depending on the type of coverage and the way that it is purchased. We've seen that group rates are often set higher by insurance companies when there is a significant number of older workers in the group. Other companies provide group insurance at progressively higher rates based on the age of the worker. Costs do come down, however, when people reach age 65 because Medicare takes over primary responsibility for coverage.

Q: Are there any research studies that demonstrate the benefit to companies from hiring and retaining older workers?

A: In a 1990 study of three companies that recruited older people, Days Inn, B & Q (a chain of home supply stores in England), and the Travelers Corporation all needed to find enough workers to handle their business. Their experience with recruits over fifty has been spectacularly successful. The British firm, for example, found that absenteeism fell by 39 percent and internal theft was 50 percent lower at the store where the older workers were placed. Profits at that same store were 18 percent higher than at the other stores. Figures covering the experience of the other two companies in the survey were similarly impressive.

> "It is time I stepped aside for a less experienced and less able man."
> —Professor Scott Elledge, on his retirement from Cornell

Q: I am a seventy-year-old cook who is fit as a fiddle in every way. I would like to go back to work. My wife thinks I am crazy, but I think there are lots of us "oldies" who could contribute a lot. Do you know any statistics on the number of older Americans who are currently unemployed who would like to work?

A: A 1993 report by the Commonwealth Fund, entitled "The Untapped Resource," found that an astonishing 5.4 million Americans over age fifty-five want to work but cannot find jobs. The same report states that one-half of those aged fifty to sixty-four who were planning to retire would stay on the job for years more if employers offered more flexible arrangements. (See Figure 4.4.) Our suggestion to you is to go ahead and try to land a job.

Q: Some of my best workers are getting close to retirement age. I'd like to make the transition as smooth as possible for all of us, and maybe even see if there are ways I can keep some of them on. What are cutting-edge strategies to achieve these ends?

A: As the number of people at the younger end of the age scale diminishes, and as companies get more inventive about meeting the needs of older workers they'd like to retain, we expect to see quite a few new initiatives emerge. To date the trend seems to be toward older workers continuing to be employed, but in job descriptions and time configurations that are alternatives to the traditional forty-hours-a-week, fifty-two-weeks-a-year option. Some organizations are bringing back retired workers during peak periods—for example, around tax time in accounting firms. Another approach involves transferring employees to less stressful functions for their last two to five years of full-time employment and permitting them to use a portion of their on-the-job time to develop skills they can use after retirement. Polaroid Corporation allows older workers to take a three-month "leave" to try out retirement, then return to work with a clearer idea of how to prepare for what lies ahead. An effective but simple strategy is to allow employees to prepare for retirement by gradually reducing their workweek. This gives both the employee and the work group a chance to explore rebalancing the workload to meet everyone's needs, and it may evolve into a steady-state reduced schedule for the older worker that can preclude the need for total retirement at this point.

Q: It's a new world out there—technology has taken over! Can older workers really cope effectively with things like computers?

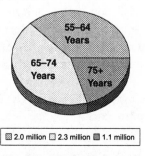

Fig. 4.4 Number of Americans Age 55 and over Who Are Willing to Work
Source: Harris Poll, 1992

A: Since eight out of ten jobs now require computer skills, these skills really are a must for all members of the workforce. If older workers lack these skills, it may be because they never had a chance to learn them. Obviously these employees completed their formal education well before schools began computer training, and many have held specialized jobs or worked in situations in which other employees entered data. Although some older workers may be fearful of computers at first, programs such as AgeWorks, cosponsored by IBM and the New York City Department for the Aging, have had excellent results in providing training in computer skills to this group. As a bonus, when older workers add these new-found technical skills to the compendium of communication and interpersonal skills that they possess, their potential value as employees is enormously enhanced. It would seem that if you want the best of all possible worlds in your employee population, it behooves you to offer your older workers a chance to get computer savvy!

Q: OK, maybe you can teach older workers some new skills. But aren't they still likely to be a little rigid and inflexible? I need team players who can "go with the flow."

A: Employers who attended last year's "Ability Is Ageless" job fair, sponsored annually by the New York City Department of Aging, reported that they are enthusiastic about hiring older workers because these workers *are* flexible. Karen Shaffer, director of AgeWorks/Senior Employment Services of the New York City Department for the Aging, explains, "They can work a variety of hours because they don't have young children at home who require their attention." And many older workers report to us that they enjoy the benefits of scheduling flexibility, as they have multiple interests in their lives and want time to pursue them.

Q: My business is fast paced. It's a go-getter environment in which people move and act quickly. Can older employers really keep up the pace?

A: We heard about one organization that believed that older employees were poor telephone salespeople because of their pacing. When they monitored telephone sales conversations conducted by employees of various ages, they noted that older workers stayed on the phone longest and, hence, made the fewest calls. They concluded that these employees were just too slow to do the work. In a surprising finding, however, an analysis of rates of sales per worker revealed that these same older workers were the most successful! It seems that the reason their conversations were longer was that they were turning noes into yeses by investing the effort to find out why the sale was nixed initially. In addition, they also got their numbers up by using their savvy to spot potential high-return accounts. The moral of this story: Question your assumptions. You may be in a fast-paced business, but that doesn't mean that older employees can't adapt and be successful. Think about what you are trying to achieve, not just what has always seemed the only the way to get there. The new, creative approaches to old problems generated by people with a slightly different perspective may just improve the bottom line.

Q: I'm nineteen and I've been working in retail, on a part-time and now a full-time basis, since I was 14. All the other salespeople treat me like a kid. I know for a fact that I am better informed, more professional, and harder working than any of them! How can I get my bosses to see me as I am?

A: If some of your work history was at other stores or if your manager is relatively new, your manager may not be aware of your track record. Set up a time to discuss your career aspirations and your performance with your boss. Explain your background as well as your hopes for promotion. On a daily basis, be sure to dress and act in a mature fashion. Perception of you as a seasoned professional, on the part of your colleagues as well as your superiors, will also enhance your career prospects.

Q: One of the benefits of my work in the physical plant department of a university is that I can take courses for free. I've always wanted to get an MBA, but I'm fifty-eight. Should I even consider doing it?

A: Go ahead! It sounds as if you might really enjoy it, and pursuing further education also sends an important signal to your employer that you are vital and up to date.

ACTION STEPS THAT WORK

1. Trust in self-selection. Most organizations have found that those employees that managers want to see retire early usually do.
2. Bring in people from your EAP or a local employment group to talk to you and your colleagues about older employees in the workplace.
3. Encourage older employees to take advantage of ongoing training. If they refuse, sit down and explore their thinking. Let them understand how crucial a choice this may be.
4. Ask your organization about developing a phase-down plan for older workers.
5. Have a career conversation with each older worker every year.

CREATING COMPETITIVE ADVANTAGE

Do's	Don'ts
• Do speak up if you hear disrespectful comments about older workers.	• Don't assume that older workers cannot get along well with their juniors.
• Do include older workers in your consideration when you have a job to fill or a promotion to make.	• Don't cling to stereotypes about older people, such as that older workers are set in their ways.
• Do provide older workers with the opportunity for further training.	• Don't deal with older workers as a class; deal with them as individuals.
• Do remember that the way you and your company treat older workers today will be how you will be treated tomorrow.	• Don't avoid dealing with performance problems of older workers.

Resources

Organizations

American Association of Retired Persons (AARP), Worker Equity Department, 601 E Street, N.W., Washington, DC 20049; (202) 434-2041. This organization, perhaps the nation's largest, with some 35 million members, provides much information of interest to business. Its newsletter, *Working Age,* is published every two months and is sent free of charge to companies interested in employment issues that affect people who are middle-aged and older. Ten regional offices across the country also provide information and assistance with employment issues.

"The Legal A,B,C's of Hiring Older Workers" is available from AARP without charge. AARP also makes available free of charge "Age Equity in Employment: A Checklist for Employers," a series of questions useful for assessing company practices.

In addition, AARP sponsors the National Older Worker Information System (NOWIS), the nation's first computerized system cataloging more than 180 private-sector employment programs to help employers expand opportunities for older workers.

The Conference Board, 845 Third Ave., New York, NY 10022; (212) 339-0390.

Operation A.B.L.E., 36 South Wabash Ave., Chicago, IL 60603; (312) 782-3335. This agency was the first in a network of eight affiliated A.B.L.E. (Ability Based on Long Experience) agencies covering various parts of the country, including Hawaii and both Northern and Southern California.

Books

Helen Dennis, *Fourteen Steps in Managing an Aging Work Force,* Lexington, MA: Lexington Books, 1988.

A. E. P. Fyock and Catherine D. Fyock, *America's Work Force Is Coming of Age: What Every Business Needs to Know to Recruit, Train, Manage, and Retain an Aging Work Force,* Lexington, MA: Lexington Books, 1990.

Olivia S. Mitchell, ed., *As the Workforce Ages,* Ithaca, NY: ILR Press, 1993.

The Untapped Resource: The Final Report of the Americans over 55 at Work Program, The Commonwealth Fund, One East 75th Street, New York, NY 10021; (212) 249-1276.

ARTICLES

"Do Age Stereotypes Influence Management Decisions?" *Working Age: An AARP Newsletter About the Changing Work Force*, Vol. 7, No. 2, July/August 1991, p. 1.

Michele Galen, "Myths about Older Workers Cost Business Plenty," *Business Week*, Dec. 20, 1993.

Walter Kiechel, "How to Manage Older Workers," *Fortune*, Nov. 5, 1990, p. 183.

AUDIOVISUAL

No Gray Areas, 26 min., Bureau of Business Practice; available from Videolearning Resource Group, (800) 648-4336.

The Power of Diversity: Module IV, Reverse Discrimination and Ageism, CorVision Media, 1359 Barclay Blvd., Buffalo Grove, IL 60089; (800) 537-3130.

CHAPTER 5

RELIGION

THE SUBJECT

"I really loved that créche we used to set up outside the plant at Christmastime. The neighbors really loved the animals as well. Now they've taken it down because of complaints from Jews. Can't we even have holiday decorations anymore?"

America is one of the most diverse countries in the world in terms of the religious affiliation of its people. In the beginning there were the rich spiritual traditions of native Americans. There were Spanish Catholics who arrived as early as the sixteenth century. Many of the Protestants from Western Europe came in search of religious freedom. Africans, brought here as slaves, came with their primarily tribal and animistic religions. Immigration continued in the mid-nineteenth century with a large influx of Roman Catholics from Ireland and, in the late nineteenth century, many Eastern Orthodox from the Balkans, Roman Catholics from southern Europe, and Jews from Russia. Approximately three decades later, many Japanese began arriving on the West Coast, bringing with them their religion, Buddhism and Shinto. Immigration to the United States has continued to this day, bringing many religions from Asia (Buddhism, Confucianism, Hinduism) and the Middle East. In fact, Muslims are the fastest-growing religious group in America; it is estimated that by the year 2000 they will number about 6 million.

The American religious landscape today is an incredible patchwork of religious denominations, splinter groups, and cults. Even among the long-established religious groups, rich diversity prevails. Protestants are divided into dozens of denominations, and Catholics, as well, are far from monolithic, with liberal and conservative groups as well as various national churches. Jews are divided into Orthodox, Conservative, Reformed, and Reconstructionist, and within these major groupings are further divisions, which often differ from one another in practice and belief. (See Figure 5.1.)

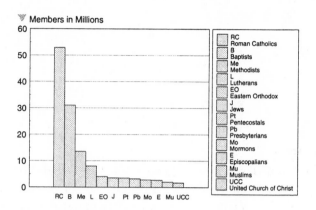

Fig. 5.1 The 12 Largest Religious Groups in the U.S.
Source: N. Y. Public Library Desk Reference, 1989.

Furthermore, new denominations and groups are emerging all the time. For example, the Church of the New Song was founded in 1970 by a convicted felon who evangelized among his fellow prisoners. Besides Judaic/Christian denominations, there are thousands of people who espouse a "New Age" kind of spirituality. They are less apt to participate in an institutional church, but they may take part in a wide array of practices ranging from meditation to conversing with spiritual beings through a channel. In addition to the adherents of all these religions and denominations, large and small, there are millions of other people who are nonpracticing or nonbelievers. Still, a huge majority of Americans, 89 percent, have a definite religious preference. (See Figure 5.2.)

"We are a nation of many nationalities, many races, many religions—bound together by a single unity, the unity of freedom and equality. Whoever seeks to set one nationality against another, seeks to degrade all nationalities. Whoever seeks to set one race against another seeks to enslave all races. Whoever seeks to set one religion against another seeks to destroy all religion."
—FRANKLIN D. ROOSEVELT, ADDRESS, NEW YORK, NOV. 1, 1940

The trend toward increasing religious diversity continues, fueled by conversions as well as immigration. Since 1957, the Christian population (Catholics and Protestants) in the United States has dropped from 92 percent to 81 percent of all persons, while practitioners of other religions, including Buddhists, Hindus, and Muslims, have increased from 1 percent to 6 percent of the population. (See Figure 5.3.) For example, there are now twenty mosques in the Islamic

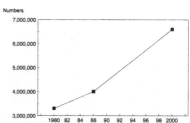

Based on the projected continuation of the 21 percent increase in total numbers of Muslims between 1981 and 1986.

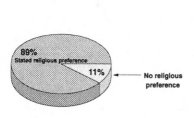

Fig. 5.2 Religious Preference in the U.S.
Source: U.S. Bureau of Labor Statistics.

Fig. 5.3 Growth of Muslims in the U.S.
Source: Yvonne Yazbeck Haddad, *The Muslims of America,* 1991.

Council of New England. And there are more than twenty-five Buddhist communities in the Boston area. In Chicago today, there are more Muslims than Methodists, more Hindus than Congregationalists, and more Buddhists than Episcopalians. Truly, this country is an amazing potpourri of religions, denominations, sects, cults, and practices.

The workforce in America reflects this incredible religious diversity. Religious belief in the workplace, however, is like the proverbial iceberg: It is often mostly invisible to the observer. Religion is an aspect of people's lives that frequently remains private and unseen. For many people, it is not an easy topic to discuss, and there are many work environments in which mentioning one's religion is taboo. There are vast variations in norms concerning religion in different geographical locations. In central Pennsylvania, for example, the Amish and some other Pennsylvania Dutch sects cling to their traditional practices and garb. In the rural South and regions of the midwestern states, Baptists and Methodists often predominate and may set a tone in the workplace far different from that in metropolitan locations. With such an incredible variety of practices and beliefs, managers must inevitably cope with an array of situations, predictable and unpredictable, that arise in a workplace that has employees with diverse religious affiliations.

"There are more things in heaven and earth, Horatio, than are dreamt of in your philosophy."
—WILLIAM SHAKESPEARE, *HAMLET*

THE LAW

Title VII of the Civil Rights Act of 1964 makes it unlawful to discriminate against employees or applicants on the basis of their religious beliefs. According to guidelines published by the federal Equal Employment Opportunity Commission, Title VII also "creates an obligation to provide reasonable accommodation for the religious practices of an employee or prospective employee unless to do so would create an undue hardship." Accommodation can mean using voluntary substitutes for certain tasks, offering flexible scheduling, or transferring an employee from one assignment to another.

> "Congress shall make no law respecting an establishment of religion, or prohibiting the free exercise thereof."
> —CONSTITUTION OF THE UNITED STATES, FIRST AMENDMENT, 1791

The guidelines specifically address the accommodation of religious practices that do not permit an individual to join or pay dues to a labor organization as well as "practices concerning dietary requirements, dress, and other grooming habits, observation of a mourning period for a deceased relative, and prohibition of medical examinations." The commission considers the "cost of accommodation in relation to the size and operating cost of the employer, and the number of employees who actually need the accommodation."

The guidelines do not limit the definition of religious practices to traditional religious beliefs, they also include moral and ethical beliefs. Under the guidelines, a belief "is religious not because a religious group professes that belief, but because the individual sincerely holds that belief with the strength of traditional religious views."

COMMON ISSUES AND CONCERNS

Here are the three issues concerning religion in the workplace that managers have mentioned to us most frequently.

SCHEDULING

Workplace schedules in the United States today typically reflect the Christian calendar. Time off is usually allotted for Christmas; holidays for non-Christians are usually not officially noted. Many companies deal with this issue by granting only legally recognized federal and state holidays as company holidays. All others—Good Friday, Rosh

Hashana, Ramadan observances, etc.—must be taken as vacation days, thus minimizing the likelihood of unequal treatment on the manager's part. However, managers may inadvertently schedule important work events on holy days of Buddhists, Muslims, Jews, or others. This is a commonly reported problem. Some managers wonder if it is wrong to schedule a strategic planning session on, say, Yom Kippur. More frequently, managers are quite oblivious to the conflicts they may be creating for employees.

OUR COMMENT

Since there is such an extensive array of religions, it is not practical for managers to try to learn about each religion and what its key holy days are. Even if they could do so, managers might not be aware of the religious affiliations of all members of their workgroup.

Managers can, however, raise the possibility of such conflicts with their workgroup in *advance*; they can indicate their willingness to attempt to respond to different religious needs. They can also, at the same time, put the responsibility for alerting them to any impending religious scheduling conflicts on the shoulders of their employees. Managers need to be flexible in granting time off for religious observances, but they need not be afraid—in this or other areas—to enter into a conversation in order to explore whether other factors are also relevant to a particular situation.

LANGUAGE

There are two types of offensive language related to religious beliefs: intentional and unintentional. Both cause hurt and anger; however, the former is cause for disciplinary action, the latter for education. If a manager fails to use one of these two tools, it indicates tacit acceptance and agreement. Some terms are patently offensive, as, for example, when people in certain religious groups are referred to in stereotypical and negative ways. Anti-Semitic comments, as well as put-downs of various other groups such as Mormons or born-again Christians are still heard in the workplace of the 1990s.

OUR COMMENT

Because it is disrespectful to all workers, whether or not they are members of the particular group in question, offensive language must be confronted by managers each time it is encountered. This can be done privately, so as not to embarrass the offender, or publicly, to make a statement to all those who are within earshot.

More difficult to anticipate is the range of individual sensitivities related to religious belief. Like scheduling conflicts, these areas of potential offense may be invisible to the manager, yet he or she needs to acknowledge and respond to conflicts as they arise. For example, some people are made uncomfortable by swearing, others by explicit sexual references or negative comments about religion in general. Ideally, managers should address this issue in a workgroup discussion prior to an actual conflict. Communication styles that offend, intentionally or accidentally, negate the concept of interpersonal connection, since people tune out when they are angry or hurt. Workplace language norms must be negotiated periodically in every work site and will shift depending on the comfort of the existing members of the workgroup.

RELIGIOUS PRACTICE

As in the case of scheduling, many of our workplace norms reflect a Western, Christian orientation. Some also reflect the norms of white males, who, until relatively recently, made up most of the inhabitants of the executive suites where the rules of dress and behavior evolved. However, in today's workforce, where employees come from a wide variety of religious traditions, their dress may present much greater variety.

While the IBM days of white shirts and no facial hair for men are history in most organizations, the range of acceptable appearance is still typically pretty narrow. Managers are not sure what kind of latitude is appropriate and what is too much. In the 1990s, for example, there may be concerns about such things as employees wearing chadors or turbans. Hairstyles such as dreadlocks can be problematic.

According to what the federal Equal Employment Opportunity Commission discovered during its public hearings on religious discrimination in New York, Milwaukee, and Los Angeles, the most common dilemmas in the workplace caused by employees' religious practices are:

- A need for a prayer break during working hours
- The practice of following certain dietary requirements

- The practice of not working during a mourning period for a deceased relative
- A prohibition against medical examinations

OUR COMMENT

This is a broad—and difficult—area. Sensitivity coupled with give and take may be required on all sides, and it is important to sort out the key issues (such as those that affect workflow) from the trivial (does it really matter that the file clerk has a pierced nose?). We see no right or wrong answers to many of these dilemmas; rather, there are approaches that are more likely to work than others. We see all these dilemmas as calling for conversation and exploration, with the focus being kept on whether the work is being negatively affected.

We urge you to keep focused on the overall job performance. If the job is being done well, you may allow flexibility for religious practice. If the job is not adequately performed, it is probably not an effect of the practice, in any case.

WORKING EXAMPLES

RAMADAN REVISITED

A major manufacturing company in the western part of the country was conducting a leadership seminar for its top 125 managers. The seminar was seven days long, and involved being away from home. When Stefan Kardorac, a young Muslim man, received his announcement about the leadership program, he immediately went to his manager, Joe Byrnes, and stated, "I can't go to the program. It's Ramadan at that time, and this means I will be fasting every day until sunset. I don't think it's a good idea for me to attend the workshop. Please take my name off the list."

Joe discovered that many other managers were also asking to be excused from the program, so he met with each of them to discuss their situations. They had all sorts of reasons why they should not attend, such as, "My wife doesn't like me to travel" and "I attended a similar seminar five years ago." During the discussions, Joe assessed each objection and either approved it or overrode it, explaining his rationale to each employee. Joe also sat down with Stefan and explored his concerns.

OUR COMMENT

As it turned out, Stefan reported to Joe that he was used to working during Ramadan. What emerged was that Stefan was scared of being at the meeting with people he didn't know very well. With a bit of gentle encouragement, he agreed to go to the program and ended up having a good experience. Ramadan, by the way, is a month-long period in the Muslim calendar during which Muslims do not eat or drink between sunrise and sunset. This example illustrates the need to look carefully into the merits of each situation. Don't make automatic decisions without getting a deeper understanding of what is going on. In this case, it really was a communication problem, not a religious one.

ACCOMMODATION—HOW MUCH IS TOO MUCH?

Joel Leibowitz is an orthodox Jew who was hired as a software engineer in a mid-sized high-tech company. At his employment interview, he explained that he would have to leave early on Friday afternoons and that there were certain holidays when he could not work. October was going to be particularly difficult that year, with seven holidays. His company agreed to this flexibility in his scheduling, but in October, his workgroup missed an important deadline. His coworkers claimed it was due in large part to Joel's being out for seven days.

Other issues arose, as well. First, Joel's workgroup had a tradition of going out to lunch for birthdays. When Joel's birthday rolled around, he explained that he could eat only in kosher restaurants, and that there were none of these nearby. Finally, his group decided to honor him by giving him a plant. His manager asked, "Though Joel is an excellent and much-respected worker, aren't there any limits to accommodation?"

OUR COMMENT

In this example, we see a critical issue (absenteeism) and a sensitive, but less important issue (the birthday celebration). Joel's absence posed a real threat to the manager's productivity. The manager must work out a course of action that will not jeopardize the whole workgroup and try to accommodate Joel's religious practices at the same time. What the manager actually did in this case was to hire a temporary worker at those times (twice a year) when Joel's absence had the most potential for upsetting the workflow. We do believe that, in general, employees should be willing to make up time lost as a result of their religious beliefs. With regard to the birthday dilemma, the workgroup solution of substituting a plant for the luncheon sounds like a creative resolution to a sticky situation.

THE PSYCHIC SPEAKS OUT

Joan Appleton, who is part of the management team in a marketing group, has been fairly open about her New Age beliefs. She often wears a crystal around her neck and shares with her colleagues information about her occasional visits to a psychic. This caused no problem for her coworker, Tom Murphy, until one day Joan announced that her psychic had told her that their approach to their major new product was mistaken and Joan strongly recommended that they change their plans significantly. Tom was highly invested in the current plan for the product and was outraged by Joan's suggestion. Tom said to Joan, "You are crazy" and went immediately to his manager, Shelly Silverstein, to complain.

> "The heart has its reasons which reason knows nothing of."
> —BLAISE PASCAL, PENSÉES

OUR COMMENT

This situation is a particularly difficult one, and we are not in total agreement about what Shelly should have done. Two of us felt strongly that Joan was out of line in bringing the opinions of her psychic into the workplace decision-making process. We identified with Tom and his concern for "rational, data-based" decisions. Another of us recognized that most of us are not the "rational man" or "rational woman" of the theoretical world and wanted to protect Joan's right to speak from her belief and experience. We all agreed that Shelly should counsel Joan to be more aware of Tom's discomfort, perhaps refraining in the future from mentioning her psychic's views on workplace matters. And Tom should be sensitive to Joan and not insult her psychic or Joan's practice.

QUESTIONS AND ANSWERS

Q: There is a woman in our company who is currently passing out literature about her religion to coworkers. I am her manager, and I am concerned. I think others are upset too. What should I do?

A: We suggest that you sit down with your evangelizing employee and have a talk. Tell her that this is not appropriate behavior in the workplace because it may create a hostile environment for others. It is not a question of freedom of speech, but rather of courtesy and consideration for colleagues. It may also be against corporate policy. Check this out with Human Resources.

Q: My family and I don't go to church. Almost everyone here at my company attends church. I am sure that the reason I did not get promoted is because I don't go. Is this discrimination?

A: We can't tell whether it's discrimination or not. We suggest that you talk to your manager and express your concern through appropriate organizational channels. Ask if the company has written criteria for advancement. Ask for specific feedback on why you were passed over. Going to church should not be a criterion unless you work at an institution that has a religious affiliation. Subtle issues such as collegial relationships and organizational individual "fit" often do figure into promotion decisions and can make this issue hazy. We counsel you to find out what happened before you jump to the conclusion that it was discrimination. Although it is unlikely that you will hear an official admission that going to church is used as a criterion for promotions, your expressed concern will raise the visibility of the issue and may result in its being reconsidered by your organization.

Q: My company has always had a Christmas tree. This year I was told that we were eliminating it because some people don't celebrate Christmas. Isn't this going too far?

A: Many companies are rethinking the whole subject of Christmas. Some are cutting out specific Christmas decorations like trees or créches. We suggest that it makes sense, in a multicultural world, to be aware of the fact that many are *not* Christians. Some companies decide to have both a Christmas tree and a menorah. In our opinion, this can get a bit complicated.

Q: I'm in charge of our annual picnic. The man who's always been assigned the responsibility for food has volunteered to take this role again, however, he's selected the same menu for as long as any of us can remember: hot dogs, hamburgers, chips, beer, and colas. It seems to me that quite a number of folks on our staff may not find one or more of these acceptable. Should I say something or just go with "tradition"?

A: Speak up—there are lots of employees who'll be grateful that someone thought of their dietary needs! These days people are on all sorts of food regimens for all kinds of reasons, ranging from political or religious beliefs to health and fitness concerns. Suggest adding non-meat items, kosher hot dogs, vegetable-based meat replacement foods, fish, and an array of veggie dishes to satisfy a wide range of appetites. Beverages should include non-caffeinated as well as non-alcoholic options. If your volunteer food coordinator needs assistance in broadening the menu, suggest he draft a few knowledgeable folks to his committee to help ease the transition.

Q: We've always enjoyed having "pools" in our office—we have regularly bet on everything from the date someone's baby would arrive to the annual Super Bowl outcome. Now one of our colleagues has announced he's Pentecostal, and that what he calls our "gambling" offends him. So we have to stop what has been a really fun part of our office routine?

A: Actually, there are several facets to this issue. First of all, is what you've been doing actually sanctioned by your organization's policies? (Many companies expressly prohibit this type of activity on site.) If, in fact, you are not violating any rules, you need to think in terms of feelings. Perhaps you might speak with your offended colleague to determine specifically what bothers him about your activities. He might find it tolerable to live with your continuing to have pools if they are more low key—for instance not celebrated and conducted via the office bulletin boards. This is an excellent example of both sides needing to compromise if we are going to be able to allow for substantial differences of viewpoint in the workplace.

Q: The woman in the cubicle next to mine has a four inch cru-cifix prominently displayed above her desk. This seems inappropriate and makes me uncomfortable. Should I ask my boss to ask her to remove it?

A: This is another of those quandaries where there is no clear right and wrong. On the one hand, it's her cubicle. On the other, you may need to be in your colleague's space period-ically to conduct business. In general, in situations like this one, we use the rule that if it doesn't infringe upon some-one else's rights, let the difference stand. It's tricky business to begin to "censor" office decor: there are, however, sorts of decoration (pornographic pictures, for example) which would be clearly inappropriate and require sanction. In this instance, we'd suggest that you inform your coworker that you'd prefer to conduct business between you in your office, or some other neutral location. If she inquires as to why, tell her clearly but gently that you are made uncomfortable by her choice to display religious icons in a business location, and that, while you are happy to work with her, you'd pre-fer a location which didn't distract you from the task at hand.

Q: I work for a small business that has three support personnel (of which I am one) working in a tiny shared space. One of my co-workers is a Christian Scientist. About three days ago, she arrived at work with a terrible cough, and she has been continuing to hack and wheeze ever since. I don't want to catch what she has—but I know she won't go to the doctor for religious reasons. What are my options?

A: This isn't really a question about religion…it's about germs and consideration for others. While your coworker may hold religious tenets which preclude her visiting a doctor, you have a right to expect that if a colleague is contagious, she'll not come to work and expose others to her illness. You need to talk to her about this problem, or, if necessary, ask your boss to intervene.

Q: My staff is approximately half Jewish and half Christian. Each year, the Jewish staff people take off three extra days for their religious holidays. This inevitably causes some grumbling among the non-Jews. I don't want to come down on anybody for celebrating their religion, but on the other hand, this is becoming a problem.

A: A lot of enlightened employers have begun to accommodate their diverse workers by going to a system of total time off. What this means is that instead of having sick days, vacation days, holidays, and personal days each accounted separately, all of an employee's available days are pooled, for him or her to take as he or she wishes. This would mean that staff members could elect to take the Jewish holidays (or any other days, for that matter) by drawing the time from their pool of days. And no one else needs to feel short-changed. We'd strongly urge you to consider this option, as it also effectively accommodates elder and child care emergencies, personal situations, and other formerly difficult to manage time off.

Q: My religion taught me that homosexuality is wrong. Against my wishes, my boss hired a woman with whom I will be expected to work closely who is open about her lesbianism. How can I be expected to work shoulder to shoulder with someone I believe is engaged in sinful behavior?

A: Just as hiring must be done on the basis of work-related attributes alone, collegial relationships must be established and maintained without regard for non-work-related characteristics. An individual's personal lifestyle, sexual preference, political views, etc. are not, in most instances, work related and should not be issues. Of course you have the right to set limits on the nature of non-work-related conversation in which you engage, and no one can force you to become friends with any coworker. You must, however, afford her professional courtesy and sufficient good will to permit both of you to succeed at what you are there for: work.

ACTIONS STEPS THAT WORK

1. Remember, in dealing with problems stemming from religious belief or practice, that the key words are "work related." Is a behavior or comment interfering with the work or is it creating a hostile environment for someone? If so, deal with it. If not, sit back.
2. Make it easy for people to complain. Be sure you are not punitive when they do complain. Many problems, if responded to, quickly evaporate.
3. Make a calendar for the year ahead. Circulate for staff additions, revisions of important dates, holidays, etc. Distribute final copy to everyone in your workgroup.
4. Review your practices around holidays to be sure you are not causing bad feelings.

CREATING COMPETITIVE ADVANTAGE

Do's	Don'ts
• Do create a work climate in which people will speak up about their individual needs vis-à-vis religion. • Do set the right tone by speaking up if someone makes an offensive comment about a religion in your presence. • Do show respect for religious differences by raising the possibility that employees will have varying religious practices and celebrate different holidays. Urge people to let you know if they have conflicts.	• Don't make any assumptions about who is what religion or what belonging to a certain religion may mean. • Don't let slurs or offensive jokes go unmentioned. You need to state your position publicly and unequivocally. • Don't make fun of anyone's religious beliefs or practice, don't tell jokes about the Pope, Jewish jokes, jokes about Holy Rollers, etc.

RESOURCES

AGENCIES

Workplace of Difference: Anti-Defamation League of B'nai B'rith, 823 United Nations Plaza, New York, NY 10017; (212) 490-2525.

The Equal Employment Opportunity Commission (EEOC), Room 4002, 2401 E Street, NW, Washington, DC 20506; (202) 634-7060. The EEOC guidelines help employers understand and interpret the law. To get a copy of these guidelines, write the EEOC.

The National Conference (founded in 1927 as the National Conference of Christians and Jews), 71 Fifth Ave., New York, NY 10003; (212) 206-0006.
- Has more than sixty regional offices throughout the United States
- Conducts diversity workshops

The Pluralism Project: World Religions in America, Project Director: Professor Diana L. Eck, Harvard University, Committee on the Study of Religion, Phillips Brooks House, Cambridge, MA 02138; (617) 495-5781, Fax: (617) 496-5798.

Southern Teaching Tolerance Program: Poverty Law Center, P.O. Box 2087, Montgomery, AL 36102; (205) 264-0286.

ARTICLES

"Religious Discrimination: Arbitrating the Grievance," *Dispute Resolution Journal*, Vol. 48, No. 4, December 1993, pp. 54–63.

"One Nation Under Gods" (religious diversity in the United States, special issue), *Time*, Fall 1993. vol. 142, no. 21, p. 62.

BOOKS

J. Gordon Melton, *Encyclopedia of American Religions*, 4th ed., Detroit: Gale Research, 1993.

AUDIOVISUALS

The Diversity Series: Race, Ethnicity, Language and Religion Workplace Issues, 20 min., Quality Media Resources, 10929 So. East 23rd St., Bellevue, WA 98004.

CHAPTER 6

FOREIGN-BORN—ETHNICITY

THE SUBJECT

IN the fall of 1993, President Clinton signed the North American Free Trade Agreement (NAFTA) into law, allowing for the easier flow of goods and services between the United States, Canada, and Mexico. In 1992, twelve European countries became a single economic market. In Asia, a similar pact called ASEAN is being developed. Borders between countries are becoming more fluid, and many of our business transactions take place across national lines. Along with the freer movement of business has come increased movement of people. In the past fifteen years, emigration to the United States has increased dramatically, as economic conditions remain difficult in many regions of the world and civil strife and ethnic conflict affect many others.

The foreign-born population in the United States reached 19.8 million in 1990. These people came from over 100 different countries.[1] Actually, America is a country in which everyone but the Native American is an immigrant. But newcomers have often been met with hostility in spite of valiant efforts to assimilate into the mainstream culture. In the past, many Americans bristled at the thought of more Italians or more Jews or more Irish arriving. In the nineteenth century, laws were passed attempting to stem the tide of foreign-born into the country. And once again, in the 1990s, strong anti-immigrant sentiments continue to erupt from time to time.

Today, despite the assimilation into the mainstream of the vast majority of these immigrants, some people whose grandparents or great-grandparents came from other countries are still strongly connected to the culture and traditions of those places. Ethnicity is one dimension of diversity that makes a great deal of difference to some people in some workplaces and very little to other people in other settings.

---

[1] Lloyd H. Rogler, "International Migrations," *American Psychologist*, August 1994, p. 701.

For example, in one public utility in New England, the senior managers had always been men who were Irish by ethnicity. It was a major event when, in the late 1980s, a man of Italian origin became a vice president. In another place, that might have passed unnoticed.

Ethnicity, by the way, refers to a group of people who are racially or historically related and who have a common and distinctive culture. Norwegians, the Masai in Kenya, and Serbs are all ethnic groups. So are people of Italian origin living in Chicago or the Kurds in northern Iraq. In this chapter we will focus primarily on issues involving people in the workplace who are foreign-born. We will also touch lightly on issues affecting workers of various ethnic groups who may or may not have been born in this country.

Today, the majority of immigrants are arriving from Latin America, Asia, and Eastern Europe, with the numbers of immigrants from Asia increasing most dramatically. (See Figure 6.1.) With the end of the Vietnam War, political repression in Southeast Asia, and coups and economic chaos in Africa and Latin America, more people from these regions began emigrating to the United States. In 1992, 22 percent of the immigrants who came to the United States were from Mexico, 8 percent were from Vietnam, 6.3 percent from the Philippines, 4.5 percent from the former Soviet Union, 4.3 percent from the Dominican Republic, and 4.0 percent from China.[2] (See Figure 6.2.)

Assimilation has been much more difficult for these groups of immigrants than for their predecessors. First, a significant number of them are not white, and so they continue to be distinguishable from others after years of living here. They are also, therefore, particularly vulnerable to anti-immigrant hostility. Second, many of these newcomers are Muslims, Hindus, or Buddhists—religions about which many people know little or nothing. Third, many of the new immigrants are refugees from extreme economic hardship and severe political repression.

Approximately 700,000 immigrants enter the United States legally every year, often to join family members who are already living here. In addition to these immigrants, each year about 120,000 refugees are granted immigration status and about 4,000 others are

---

[2] "The Numbers Game," *Time*, Special Issue, Fall 1993, pp. 14–15.

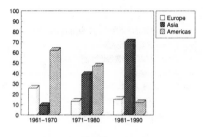

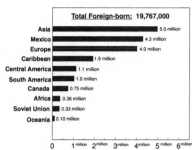

Fig. 6.1 Changing Size of Immigrant Groups as a Percentage of Total Immigrants (by Decade)
Source: U.S. Immigration and Naturalization Service, Statistical Yearbook, Annual.

Fig. 6.2 The Place of Birth of Foreign-Born Persons in the U.S.: 1990
Source: U.S. Bureau of the Census

granted political asylum.[3] Currently there are over 11 million immigrants working in America, earning over $240 billion and paying $90 billion in taxes. While the actual number of illegal aliens is unknown, the U.S. Immigration and Naturalization Service estimates that approximately 3.2 million are living in America. Other estimates run as high as 5 million illegal aliens.

These numbers have enormous implications for the U.S. workforce. A growing proportion of the workforce is foreign-born, and this proportion will increase in the decades ahead. (See Figure 6.3.) Consider the following percentages of population that are foreign born: in Los Angeles, 27 percent; in San Francisco, 20 percent; in New York, 20 percent; in Dallas, 18 percent; and in Washington, D.C., 12 percent. (See Figure 6.4.)

Many of the new arrivals to the United States from Latin America live in Hispanic enclaves. Throughout the country, over 6 million Hispanics live in these neighborhoods. Moreover, Spanish is spoken by almost all people of Hispanic origin. Therefore, there is less need for Latinos to learn English, a key factor for integration into American culture. On the other hand, Asian and African immigrants speak hundreds of different languages and dialects, making it more necessary for them to learn English to get along.

---

[3] Philip Bennett, "Fear of Newcomers Soaring Along with Immigration Levels," *Boston Globe*, April 2, 1993, p. 1.

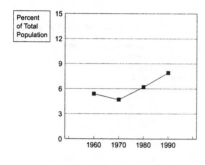

Fig. 6.3 Foreign-Born Persons as a Percentage of
Total Population
Source: U.S. Bureau of the Census

Fig. 6.4 Percentage Who Are Foreign-Born in
Major U.S. Cities
Source: U.S. Bureau of the Census

It is important not to overlook the positive reasons for hiring
people born in another country or those still influenced by the traditions and culture of their ancestors. Here are five benefits these workers offer: (1) They often bring to organizations insights from another
culture at a time when the marketplace is increasingly international;
(2) they can bring a fresh vantage point for looking at business issues;
(3) they expand the potential pool of new hires; (4) some foreign-
born bring skills that are scarce in the United States, while others provide unskilled labor, which remains necessary in our workplaces; and
(5) the foreign-born provide a mirror that allows the rest of us to better understand our own culture.

"The winners in the new borderless economy will be the brands and companies that make the best
use of richness of experience they get from their geographical diversity."
—GURCHARAN DAS, IN THE *HARVARD BUSINESS REVIEW*

THE LAW

It is illegal to discriminate against people because they are foreign-
born. Title VII of the Civil Rights Act of 1964 prohibits discrimination in the workplace based on national origin. More recent federal
legislation, the Immigration Reform and Control Act of 1986
(IRCA), extends the coverage of the law to businesses with four or
more employees. Penalties for violation of the law include reinstatement of the employee, back pay for as much as two years, and fines
for the employer.

In 1987, the Equal Employment Opportunity Commission issued guidelines that define national origin discrimination broadly as "denial of equal employment opportunity because of an individual's, or his or her ancestor's, place of origin; or because an individual has the physical, cultural, or linguistic characteristics of a national origin group." Recently, there has been an increase in the number of complaints of discrimination because of national origin. In 1989, 11,114 complaints were filed; in 1992, over 14,000 were filed.

The EEOC looks unfavorably at company rules that require employees to speak English at all times. In addition, this federal law enforcement agency disapproves of height and weight requirements for employment that might have the effect of discriminating against some foreign-born job applicants who may be much smaller on average than their American-born counterparts.

Because of the large increase in the number of immigrants arriving in America and the current economic climate, there is a widespread and growing concern about illegal aliens. Employers can get in serious trouble if they employ people who do not have the correct papers. The Federal Immigration Act of 1990 requires the employer to ask for proof that a person is a U.S. citizen or has a working card. The "green card" is highly coveted, and often employers, as well as the foreign-born themselves, spend much time and energy working through the red tape of bureaucracy to secure green cards.

COMMON ISSUES AND CONCERNS
LANGUAGE

One of the greatest challenges posed by new immigrants is language. Over 13 percent of the U.S. population speaks a language other than English at home. (See Figure 6.5.) In cities such as Miami, El Paso, and San Diego, it is just as common to hear Spanish, Creole, Portuguese, Vietnamese, and Chinese as it is to hear English. In Massachusetts, for instance, one in seven residents speaks a language other than English at home. In the Falls Church, Virginia, school district, there are over one hundred languages spoken by students.

Language can often cause friction in the workplace. Those for whom English is a second or third language may misunderstand and make mistakes. Lack of a good command of English can create the impression that these people lack intelligence and are not competent. This may well be far from the truth.

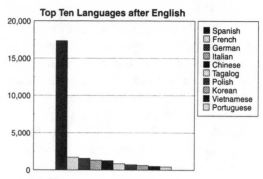

Fig. 6.5 Persons Speaking a Language Other than English at Home
Source: U.S. Bureau of the Census

"We need every human gift and cannot afford to neglect any gift because of artificial barriers of sex or race or class or national origin."
—MARGARET MEAD, *MALE AND FEMALE,* 1949

Another problem stemming from language comes when several employees speak a language other than English in the workplace. This can irritate or even infuriate others. People who would never make a racial slur feel comfortable with their anger and put down coworkers who don't speak English fluently. We frequently hear opinions such as the following: "This is America, and they should speak English." "I don't think they should be here if they don't speak English." "I'm sick of it—it's totally frustrating to try to work with people who don't speak English."

OUR COMMENT

It is important for you as a supervisor or manager to deal directly with those problems of language. First, you need to provide support to people whose language skills are poor. Find out if they are interested in learning more English. If they are, tell them about resources that can help. Many companies sponsor English as a second language (ESL) classes. For instance, subsidiaries of the H.J. Heinz Company provide company-sponsored language instruction after hours and offer tuition reimbursement to supervisors willing to learn Spanish. If an employee says that he or she doesn't want to learn more English, accept this, but explain any negative effects this may have on the work getting done or on the employee's potential for advancement.

Particularly in cases where there is only one non-English speaker, you need to work with your workgroup to create a supportive environment for him or her. Make it clear to the workgroup that you want to see assistance given to this person.

Forbidding employees to speak their primary language at any time may create, in the words of the EEOC guidelines, "an atmosphere of inferiority, isolation, and intimidation based on national origin which could result in a discriminatory working environment." We advise against this kind of policy and urge companies to take another approach. Some companies, such as US WEST, provide sales literature, applications, and contracts in Spanish. H.J. Heinz offers a program in which bilingual employees serve as "buddy" translators, and also refers recent arrivals to social service agencies for assistance in obtaining work permits and housing. Microsoft has established a network of support groups for those having trouble adapting to the new work environment. (See Figure 6.5.)

"And so the old biblical myth turns in on itself. The confusion of languages is no longer a punishment...[but is] the pleasure of the cohabitation of languages which work side-by-side...the Happy Babel."
—ROLAND BARTHES, *LE PLAISIR DU TEXTE*

ACCENTS

Not only are those who have limited fluency in English often mistreated in the workplace, but those who speak English with an accent also face a surprising degree of hostility and ridicule. Because speech is so often used to gauge intelligence, the foreign-born, if they retain even traces of their mother tongue, are judged to be stupid. Their career advancement may be significantly limited. For instance, having an accent is often mentioned as a weakness on performance reviews.

"Sometimes Americans act like they have never heard a person with an accent."
—GALO CONDE, NEW YORK PUBLIC SCHOOL TEACHER

In certain circumstances, an accent can be truly a problem. In one company where we worked, many employees agonized because one of their coworkers, an Asian-American woman, spoke such broken English. Talking to her on the telephone was frustrating for customers because she had information that was critical that they get exactly right. Even when they asked her to repeat her comments three times, they still were confused.

OUR COMMENT

When an employee cannot speak English well enough to fulfill the job description, then action must be taken. The first step is to sit down with the employee and convey the specific problems that his or her accent is creating. Then suggest several alternatives, such as changing the person's responsibilities or providing him or her with training. Often speech therapy and/or ESL classes may be required. Sometimes training for the coworkers may be the best solution. The Hillhaven Corporation, for example, conducts courses for English speakers to better listen to those with accents and to teach them basic words in widely used foreign languages.

JOKES/RIDICULE

In addition to being subjected to hostility and resentment, the foreign-born also face ridicule. Ethnic jokes are one of the most common types of humor in the workplace. We've heard Russian, Finnish, Japanese, Italian, Polish, Norwegian, English, Puerto Rican, Jewish, and French Canadian jokes in the workplace. In short, there are jokes about every ethnic group. Often it is the same joke; only the ethnic group being mocked changes. In addition, it is not unusual for employees to make fun of the mannerisms and accents of coworkers of a different ethnic group.

OUR COMMENT

Humor aimed at the foreign-born may seem harmless enough; this kind of joke is so much a part of our culture that many people have a very hard time seeing anything wrong with it. At least once, the EEOC has found a violation of law on the part of a company that allowed a Polish-born employee to be victimized by an ongoing barrage of jokes poking fun at Poles.

Just as racial, ethnic, or offensive sexual humor must not be tolerated in the workplace, ethnic jokes and ridicule of foreigners are totally inappropriate in today's multicultural work environment. You need to speak up when you hear this type of humor and put a stop to it. You can do this by saying, "That kind of joke is not appropriate," or "Cut the ethnic jokes—I find them offensive." Remember, your work-group looks to you for signals about what is okay and what is out of bounds.

"Every day, American employers are losing millions of dollars because these talents (foreign-looking or sounding employees) are frozen."
—JOY CHERIAN, EEOC COMMISSIONER

STEREOTYPES

Being stereotyped is perhaps the most pervasive problem that foreigners and employees from various ethnic groups confront. Stereotypes are a set of generalizations, which are often distortions, about the characteristics of a group. People all too often assume that every individual in a group has these characteristics without checking it out.

For example, people from Ireland are stereotyped by others as being people who fight a lot, drink a lot, and have the gift of gab. Politicians of Italian background often complain about a presumption that they have contacts with organized crime. Native Americans, though not foreign-born, also face negative stereotyping.

Even positive stereotypes can be problematic. An Asian-American working in a large bank in the Midwest told us that in her organization, Asian-Americans are seen as "hard-working, technically minded, and particularly good at math." This woman explained, "That's just not me. I got C's in algebra in high school, and have avoided math ever since."

OUR COMMENT

What makes stereotypes so difficult to deal with is their deep roots in popular culture. It's as if society has an investment in preserving ways of looking at ethnic groups.

We suggest a couple of ways you can deal with stereotypes in your workgroup. First, whenever you hear a person being stereotyped, say something like, "That's a stereotype. Let's check it out and see if it holds in this case." When you hear generalizations being made about any ethnic group you can ask, "I really wonder if all _____ s are that way."

WORKING EXAMPLES
THE GLASS CEILING

Julio Francona's family emigrated from Nicaragua five years ago and settled in a Latino community in Los Angeles. Two years ago, Julio was hired as a teller in a local branch of a large bank in his neighborhood. Because of his fluency in both Spanish and English, he was seen as a valuable asset. He could communicate with the many new arrivals to the neighborhood from Latin America as well as with other customers.

Recently, a loan officer position opened up in the main office of the bank. This was a long-awaited opportunity for Julio to advance. His performance reviews had been stellar, so he applied. Two weeks later, Julio found out that he had been denied the promotion. After discussing the situation with his manager, he learned that while he was definitely qualified for the position, those in charge of hiring felt that he was needed more at the local branch because of his language skills. No one else could do his job, and there were concerns about whether he was a good fit for the central office.

OUR COMMENT

Frequently bilingual employees are noticed primarily for their language skills; their other skills are overlooked. The concern about fit may also be a result of stereotypes. Management might have been wiser to think more about Julio's professional development than its short-term convenience. In the long run, this would have benefited both the bank and Julio.

DENIED PROMOTION

Harry Chin emigrated to Seattle from mainland China in the middle 1980s. Because Harry had an excellent engineering background and spoke English reasonably well, he quickly landed a job in a high-tech firm. It was an entry-level professional position that enabled Harry to demonstrate his intelligence and fine work habits. He proved to be a remarkably quick learner, and in a short time, he became a valued employee. Harry applied three times for a manager's job. Each time he was turned down without any explanation. Upon looking at his performance reviews, several managers had noted that although his technical skills were excellent, he rarely spoke up and did not assume a leadership role. Harry was quite confused, as he had organized and led several projects, all of which were successful.

OUR COMMENT

Overall, according to David Chai, a Chinese-American systems engineer quoted in *Business Week* on June 21, 1993, it takes Asians three to five times longer to get their first promotion than it does white males. One explanation for this fact is that many Asian-Americans are seen as preferring technical jobs rather than managerial positions.

But clearly this is not always the case. It seems as if Harry's managers were making unexamined assumptions about Harry's abilities and his career. Not only is the company at serious risk of losing Harry, but also it appears to be denying Harry an opportunity he deserves. In the *Business Week* article referred to above, AT&T Bell Laboratories reported that Asian-Americans leave Bell Labs at a rate twice that of white males.

THE CASE OF THE HARASSED IMMIGRANT

Felicia Rodriguez fled El Salvador during the civil war that raged in the 1980s. After her arrival in Dallas, she managed to learn English at a community college, acquired the basics of word processing, and was hired by a large real estate agency. As a secretary-receptionist, Felicia has proven to be an adequate employee, although she frequently arrives late to the office. Her coworkers kid her about being "emotional" and talking too much.

Behind her back, and occasionally even to her face, staff members make fun of Felicia. Once when Felicia was away on vacation, one of the realtors did a "Felicia act," wearing a flowery broadbrimmed summer hat and long, dangling earrings. Everyone, including the office manager, thought the imitation was hysterically funny. Felicia feels uneasy in the office environment, even though she is unaware that she is the butt of office humor. She wonders if she will ever feel comfortable there.

OUR COMMENT

By allowing people to make fun of Felicia, the manager has colluded in creating a hostile work environment. Felicia may have some performance problems, but the lack of respect being shown to her is inexcusable. We think the agency is ripe for some diversity awareness training, which includes taking a good hard look at stereotyping and an assessment of the office environment.

OPEN HOSTILITY

The workforce at an orange juice packaging plant in Miami is made up largely of workers whose parents came from Cuba forty years ago and Haitians who arrived more recently. A long-standing rift between the Cubans and the Haitians has poisoned the work atmosphere. The two groups refuse to work together. As a result, some of the workgroups are all Haitian and others are all Cuban. There is a lack of cooperation between the groups that has, at times, slowed down production. Recently two machines on the lines where Haitians work have broken down unexpectedly, and somewhat suspiciously. The supervisor, Nick Ives, who is Anglo, strongly suspects sabotage, though, of course, he cannot say who might have done it.

OUR COMMENT

Clearly something has to be done, as the work is not getting done. Nick feels at a loss, as he can't speak either Spanish or Creole and really doesn't understand what's going on. As a start, we suggest that he sit down with representatives from both groups and ask what they think is the problem. Getting a dialogue started is imperative. It may make sense to bring in leaders from the two communities to foster communication between the groups. Nick might also consider hiring a mediator skilled in conflict resolution to assist him.

We also recommend that Nick begin a process of learning about the people in his factory. His ignorance of their languages and of their cultures probably reduces his effectiveness. Even a few phrases of Spanish and Creole might have helped him develop greater rapport with his workers and allowed him access to critical information.

"Building a shared base of understanding takes time and we had to learn how to do that in a multilingual, multinational environment."
—DAVID WHITWAM, WHIRLPOOL CEO

QUESTIONS AND ANSWERS

Q: I work in a fast-food restaurant in southwestern Texas, and we have hired a lot of Mexicans who don't have any working papers. My boss tells me not to worry, but I do, because I know it is illegal.

A: Your company is in jeopardy and may well be fined by the Immigration and Naturalization Service, a division of the

Justice Department. You are in a tough position if your supervisor refuses to obey the law. It may be risky for you to blow the whistle or go talk to your boss's supervisor. It is a matter of conscience, but you'll have to weigh all the factors in your situation.

Q: Last week both a U. S. citizen and a legal alien applied for the same job as a welder in my plant. They both have equal qualifications, and their experience looks pretty much the same to me. I felt that I should give the nod to the citizen. Does that make sense, or have I violated the law?

A: The Immigration Reform and Control Act of 1986 says that preference can be given to the citizen. However, because the same law forbids discrimination against certain legal aliens, the situation remains murky. We recommend making a further effort to decide the case on the basis of qualifications, even if the differences between the applicants remain slight.

Q: I work in an international division of a major oil company. We bring many managers from our overseas refineries for training in the United States. Several managers from Venezuela and Nigeria who have twenty years of experience with the company have told me how upset they are because their badges say "Trainee." Why does the company treat them with so little respect?

A: Often companies are unaware of the ways in which they may be insulting people from other countries and cultures. It is impossible to anticipate all the issues with foreign employees or people from other cultures. The best way to proceed is to sit down and ask people, "How are things going?" Some companies hold employee feedback sessions where this kind of issue can surface.

Q: Our company is located in a state that recently passed a law requiring the reporting of illegal aliens. I'm a plant manager, and I have reason to believe that a substantial number of our employees are probably here illegally. I feel it would be wrong to turn them in. What should I do?

A: This is a really tough issue. It's a bit early to tell how the various constituencies will deal with legislation, but already teachers and medical personnel are taking stands against being in a reporting role. You can have an impact by working to overturn this law; in the meantime, consult (informally, if possible) with a member of your human resources department to get a sense of the way your company is going to respond to this development.

Q: I'm the director of human resources for a midwestern plastics manufacturer. There is virtually no public transportation from the city to my factory, which is located in a white, middle-class suburb. In an effort to diversify our workforce and draw on the potential immigrant employee pool in the city, I have begun running a bus between the plant and the city during commuting hours. I have begun to hear rumors of irritation and jealousy among workers who commute unassisted; apparently, some people think what I am doing is unfair. Do you?

A: We're with you on this one, and we think no apologies are necessary for your smart business strategy. All employees of your organization will benefit if your company grows strong and solid; one way to ensure this—and the employees' continued gainful employment—is to recruit the best possible workers. If it takes a little assistance in the transportation area to net you the best and the brightest, we say go for it!

Q: I'm a first-generation Italian-American, and I'm constantly overhearing jokes at work about the Mafia, organized crime, etc., that imply that Italians are gangsters and thugs. I'm a hard-working, honest guy, and I hope to succeed in my career. Is it realistic to think I can really get a fair shot here?

A: It's hard to say with such limited information about your organization. However, unless your company is unusually biased, you'll probably encounter similar stereotypes wherever you go. If you are generally happy where you are, the best strategy is probably to stay and push ahead. It is critically important that you respond to these comments when you hear them; that kind of feedback can begin to break the cycle of stereotyping. It is also important for your own self-esteem that you speak up.

Q: My high-tech company has been forced to downsize several times because of poor sales. We've been especially badly hurt by the Japanese companies that are our competition. I'm a Japanese-American, and I cringe when I hear my colleagues swearing about our Japanese competitors, using derogatory language and ethnic slurs. I'm as loyal as the next guy, and I really want our company to make it. But I'm getting genuinely uncomfortable with all the Japan bashing going on around me. Help!

A: Your loyalty both to your employer and your colleagues and to your own roots has put you in a tough spot. Hopefully, you'll be able to use your awareness to educate your coworkers. People need to hear your voice objecting to the slurs and inappropriate comments. Not taking action in these situations implies that you condone them. And you certainly don't want to do that.

Q: Our engineering firm employs a lot of Arab professionals. But recently anti-Arab jokes and comments seem to have become the norm. My wife is from the Middle East, so I feel upset whenever I hear these comments. I am afraid to speak up to my boss and the guys I work with because I am very shy. What can I say?

A: Practice a couple of all-purpose lines such as, "I find that joke offensive" or "Your comment makes me uncomfortable." This is hard to do, but it is important to create a work climate that feels welcoming to all.

ACTION STEPS THAT WORK

1. Find out what kinds of language assistance your organization and your community offer to people who want to improve their skills in English. Encourage employees who need and want these classes to attend.
2. If you have a number of workers who speak another language, suggest to Human Resources that the basic company documents get translated into that language.
3. Take a class in whatever language the people in your workplace speak.
4. Survey your workgroup about the work climate. Ask whether employees get respect regardless of their national origin.
5. If you have many people from a certain ethnic group in your workgroup, read a book or watch a video about that country/people.

CREATING COMPETITIVE ADVANTAGE

Do's	Don'ts
• Do remember that stereotypes diminish over time with day-to-day contacts.	• Don't tolerate the use of ethnic slurs such as "Spic," "Wop," "Jap," or "Polack."
• Do speak up when your hear anyone in your workgroup stereotyping another person because of his or her ethnicity.	• Don't assume that people want to be identified as belonging to a certain national or ethnic community.
• Do be wary of job requirements, such as insisting on fluent English if this is not really critical for doing the job.	• Don't ignore ethnic jokes—let people know that they are disrespectful and can hurt.
• Do ask foreign-born workers what it was like in their homeland. Many people are eager to share information about their country and culture.	• Don't create ghettos in the workplace where workers from one country are isolated from other employees.

RESOURCES

ORGANIZATIONS

The American Immigration Lawyers Association, Suite 1200, 1400 Eye Street, NW, Washington, DC 20005; (202) 371-9377. Provides expert information and monitoring on issues related to immigration, as well as the names of attorneys with expertise in these issues.

National Center for Immigrants Rights, 1550 West 6th Street, Los Angeles, CA 90017.

Immigrant Legal Resource Center, 1663 Mission St., Suite 602, San Francisco, CA 94103-2449; (415) 255-9499.

Center for Immigrants' Rights, Inc., 48 St. Marks Place, New York, NY 10003; (212) 505-6890, fax (212) 995-5876. Documents the impact of employer sanctions on citizens and immigrants. Provides training in immigration law and community education on immigration issues.

BOOKS

Austin T. Fragomen, Jr., Alfred del Rey, Jr., and Sam Bernsen, *Immigration Law and Business*, Clark Boardman and Company, Ltd., 435 Hudson Street, New York, NY 10017: Published since 1983, with annual supplements. An accessible two-volume work bound in a three-ring binder, that offers valuable information for employers.

Understanding the Immigration Act of 1990, Federal Publications, Inc. 1120 20th St. NW, Washington, DC, 20036-3484, 1991.

U.S. Immigration Made Easy 1993–94: The Insider's Guide, Sheridan Worldwide, Inc. Suite 103-392, 10105 E. Via Linda, Scottsdale, AZ 85258, 1993.

ARTICLES

Gurcharan Das, "Local Memoirs of a Global Manager," *Harvard Business Review*, March–April 1993, pp. 38–47.

James G. Frierson, "National Origin Discrimination: The Next Wave of Lawsuits," *Personnel Journal*, December 1987, pp. 97–108.

"The Immigrants: How They're Helping to Revitalize the U.S. Economy," *Business Week*, July 13, 1992, pp. 114–19.

Interpreter Releases, a weekly publication (since 1921) from the American Council for Nationalities Services, 20 West 40th Street, New York, NY 10018; it contains information important to employers.

CHAPTER 7

HIERARCHY AND CLASS

THE SUBJECT

A large financial institution was celebrating its one-hundredth anniversary with a huge party for all its officers and its board of directors in the atrium of its headquarters. In one corner of the courtyard, a band was playing. In another corner, tables were laden with fancy sandwiches, a huge ten-layer cake, and elaborate ice sculptures. Champagne corks were popping as the invited guests wandered into the courtyard. Meanwhile, peering through the windows on all sides, the uninvited employees watched the celebration. As we heard the story, some of them felt envious, like little children watching a grown-up party. Others felt wistful at having been left out. Still others reported that, as they watched, they could feel their anger mounting. Four years after this happened, we still hear dozens of versions of the story. Many of those who were not invited remember this incident with total clarity. For many of them it was an important event in shaping their relationship with the firm. No one who attended the party has ever mentioned it to us.

SECOND-CLASS CITIZENS

As the vignette about the party suggests, treating different levels of employees differently can have a significant impact. Within almost every organization there is a hierarchy among the employees that is based on position, title, role, and function. For example, in the situation described above, officer status is an important distinction that shapes an employee's entire work experience. It is not just a question of being invited to a party or not. At most corporations there is an enormous chasm between senior executives and everyone else. Some companies have many levels, like a heavy machinery manufacturing company that has twelve levels of management and ten levels of employees who are not managers below that.

Hierarchical status in the workplace typically begins with, but is not limited to, the exempt/nonexempt dynamic. People who work with their hands (say, on the manufacturing floor) often have lower status than those who work in an office setting. In some organizations, union workers are considered to be at the base of the pyramid, nonunion employees and professionals form the next layer, and management is at the top of the triangle. Certain types of organizations have pecking orders specific to the nature of the work. At many colleges and universities, for instance, the faculty occupy the top slot, administrative personnel are seen as a level below them, and students and staff are at the bottom. Clearly, the kind of job a person has places him or her somewhere in a hierarchy that is more or less clearly defined. (See Figure 7.1.)

More recently, with greater competition and the pressure to be lean, organizations have been flattening their ranks and eliminating levels of middle management. At GE, for example, many divisions have gone from 10 or 12 levels to 4 to 6 levels. There is a lot of talk about the horizontal organization replacing the traditional pyramid, but even in those so-called horizontal organizations, there are three categories of employees—the "tops," the "middles," and the "bottoms."

Internal distinctions involving status and hierarchy often create differences that are more obvious than some of the other kinds of diversity discussed in this book. Boundaries between levels can act as roadblocks to career mobility. They can also have a significant impact upon both the morale and the emotional well-being of those lower in

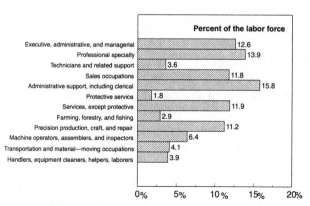

Fig. 7.1 Jobs in the U.S.: 1992
Source: U.S. Bureau of Labor Statistics.

the pecking order (see the model below). This "one up/one down" model illustrates the dynamic between levels. (See Chart 7.1.) Those higher in the hierarchy are often quite oblivious to the feelings of the "down" people and to the extent to which those below them are going out of their way to meet their needs.

"Working class life is demeaning not because its culture or values are inferior, but because of the lack of money, the lack of opportunity, lack of job responsibility, lack of respect, lack of power—i.e. because of the oppressive treatment of the working class by the higher classes."
—MARY MCKENNEY IN *QUEST,* VOL. III, NO. 4, SPRING, 1977

In this chapter, we focus on the major issues and concerns that result from hierarchical distinctions in the workplace. We will also touch briefly on the impact of "class" on the workplace. Class, as we define it, is a group of people sharing the same economic, education-al, and social background. Some people believe that the level of edu-cation attained is the most important way of differentiating one per-

CHART 7.1
ONE UP/ONE DOWN MODEL
Up Persons ...
- Feel good, satisfied with relationships.
- Experience no need to share feelings, opinions, judgments.
- Typically keep others doing all the "psyching out."
- Have needs largely met by one-down persons.
- Feel positive about the work climate.
- Are oblivious to feelings of those who are down.

Down Persons ...
- Morale suffers.
- Withhold feelings, thoughts, because of perceived risks.
- Seek support of like-kind people.
- Feel resentful, angry.
- Realize own needs are not going to be met.
- Spend a lot of time "psyching out" the up persons.
- Take care of the perceived needs of the up persons
- May lose track of own needs.
- Productivity may be reduced.

son from another. (See Figure 7.2.) Others think income is the most critical component of class distinctions. (See Figure 7.3.) What we are thinking about are the consequences in the workplace of a person coming from, for example, a working-class background compared to another person whose background might include prep school, an Ivy League education, and inherited wealth.

Sociologists assert that the United States has far fewer class distinctions than almost every other country in the world. Many people believe that class has a minimal impact in the workplace of the 1990s. Others, however, like Benjamin DeMott, who has recently written about class in America, see class as a largely unacknowledged distinction between people, but one that has some important effects on the work environment nonetheless. A 1994 *Fortune* magazine article, "Class in America," states, "To acknowledge any interest in class status or to spend much time thinking about socio-economic ranking is to behave in some vaguely un-American way."

"Upper class in America is a vague status derived mostly from the accomplishments and money of ancestors, not the living individual."
—BRIAN O'REILLY IN *FORTUNE,* JUNE 30, 1990

In the mid-nineties, the subject of class is starting to come out of the closet. Several conferences were held on the topic in 1994, and class has become part of market research. For example, Claritas, a market research company located in Virginia, divides American society into sixty-two classes, each with its own culture. It gives these groups labels like Blue-Chip, Golden Ponders, Young Subordinates, and Hard

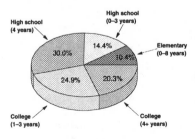

Fig. 7.2 Levels of Education in the U.S.: 1990
Source: 1990 Census

Fig. 7.3 U.S. Household Incomes: 1993
Source: The Lifestyle Market Analyst, 1993.

Scrabble. Companies target their direct mail efforts to those specific groups that are likely to buy their particular services or products.

"No longer are Americans rising and falling together as if in one large national boat. We are, increasingly, in different smaller boats."
—ROBERT REICH, SECRETARY OF LABOR, CLINTON ADMINISTRATION

We think that both hierarchy and class create differences that are important to include in this book. We are not advocating that hierarchical differences or class differences should be appreciated! This is somewhat different from our position on other dimensions of diversity, such as age, gender, race, and ethnicity, where we think having people with differences actually adds positive value for the organization. Rather, our position is that no one should be treated without respect or penalized for being at the top or at the bottom of the organizational hierarchy. And, certainly, no one should be given more advantages for coming from a background of privilege. We even wonder if it makes sense to provide additional privileges and perks to those who are at the top of the organizational ladder.

THE LAW

It is illegal to offer different retirement packages, such as different 401(k) plans, to different levels of employees. However, companies can legally create and offer different compensation and benefits packages for their managers and nonmanagerial employees, for exempt and nonexempt, and for union and nonunion. They can also have all sorts of policies about upward mobility from one job level to another and what is required to be in a certain job category.

The law is silent on the subject of class as defined by socioeconomic background or status. When someone doesn't get hired or doesn't get promoted, it would be virtually impossible to demonstrate that this was discrimination on the basis of class. Moreover, using subjective standards is not illegal per se. However, as subjective criteria can easily be used to mask prejudice and discriminatory attitudes, they have been described as "a ready mechanism for discrimination." Courts have been particularly willing to uphold the use of subjective criteria to evaluate candidates for white-collar jobs as opposed to blue-collar jobs because criteria for such jobs are more difficult to evaluate objectively in most cases.

COMMON ISSUES AND CONCERNS

Organizations vary widely in the degree to which hierarchy and class create issues for their employees and the degree to which these are recognized as problems. At some workplaces there is a steady stream of complaints involving issues of hierarchy; at others, these differences do not evoke much interest. In most organizations, issues of class are totally under the table. Here are the most common issues and concerns related to differences of hierarchy and class that have been reported to us.

PIGEONHOLED

When an organization has rigid boundaries and little interaction between support staff and professionals, between union and nonunion employees, or between senior and middle management, opportunity for career development and upward mobility can remain limited. People may be stereotyped, put in pigeonholes, and their potential for development may not be seen. Some organizations even have policies that prohibit moving from one category of job to the next.

> "The professional and managerial group is still the middle class, and its only capital is knowledge and skill."
> —BARBARA EHNENREICH, AUTHOR OF "FEAR OF FALLING," *FORTUNE*, JULY 30, 1990

For example, at one manufacturing company, policy forbids support staff moving into the ranks of administration, no matter how good their performance has been. More frequently, there is no policy that forbids promoting employees to a new kind of job in a quite different function—it just doesn't happen very often. In one public utility company, for example, it is truly rare for excellent workers who are in the union ranks to be spotted for management jobs.

OUR COMMENT

Often impermeable ceilings and walls between organizational levels and groups are taken for granted as "the way things are." Frequently, it is just the blinders of tradition and stereotyping that prevent managers and supervisors from seeing the potential of their lower-level employees. As a manager or supervisor, you may not be in a position to change the policies or redo the organizational chart. What you can do is open your eyes to the talent and potential of people in your workgroup and put in some extra effort helping every worker think about his or her career development. Sit down informally with each person in your group and talk about his or her hopes and dreams. Or better still, hold an hour-long meeting with everyone once a year to talk about career development issues and to help them plan ahead.

In addition, make the effort to get to know some employees in other parts of your organization who might be good prospects for your workgroup. This way, when an opening does come up, you are prepared. But be sure you get acquainted with some people who are different from yourself—in age, lifestyle, training, race, gender, etc.

TITLES AND PERKS

In a significant number of corporations, employees spend many hours thinking about their position on the organizational chart. People devote years trying to acquire the title of manager or vice president. For example, at one company that was restructuring, managers were drawn as boxes on the organizational chart while project leaders were triangles. Some of the triangles who wished to be boxes spent hours figuring out how they could alter their status. Many of those who had been managers before the restructuring but lost their boxes, were so bitter that they left the organization. Since they were, by and large, competent employees, it was a real loss for the organization.

Office space, office size, location, and furnishings often reflect a finely tuned gradation of perks related to organizational status. In one company, working with a group in a large, undivided space is for those at the bottom of the pecking order. Cubbies without windows are for those at the next level. As you move up the hierarchy, you get a cubby with windows and then an office with a door that closes. As you advance even higher, you get an office with windows, then a larger office, and finally the prized corner office. Some organizations have a graduated list of furniture that goes along with reaching a certain level of management. In one organization, being given a credenza was the coveted symbol of success.

OUR COMMENT

Recently, there has been a turn away from this kind of graduated perk system, as it has enormous potential to create bad feelings and to waste time and energy. At one manufacturing company in the south, management decided to do away with all reserved parking places.

After the decision, however, a number of the individual managers who had made the decision were shocked at having to give up their spaces. "You don't mean my space?" was a common refrain.

Many companies are moving away from a workplace in which the managers wear neckties while everyone else dresses more casually. At Chevron Overseas Petroleum Company in California, a Friday dress-down day was instituted. When it was clear that managers could still get their work done without wearing a suit or necktie, the company took another step and made every day dress-down day. To the amazement of some staffers, the work continued to be turned out, plus morale rose noticeably.

We think minimizing distinctions makes sense. Research informs us that employees who feel "out" or "down" rather than "in" or "up" also have less job satisfaction, less commitment, and less loyalty to their organization. As an individual manager or supervisor, you can minimize the scrambling after titles and perks by the way you behave. You might consider, for example, moving to a less desirable office space or eliminating some perks based solely on status. Managers who have tried this are often amazed at the positive results.

LIMITED OPPORTUNITY

When we ask groups of employees, "What does it take to get ahead in this organization?" we used to be surprised by the kinds of answers we got. We expected to hear about competence, commitment, technical skills, and people skills. And these are frequently mentioned. But, in addition, we almost always hear, "It depends on who you know, on being in the old-boy network." At one company in Boston, we heard, "You have to live in a town beginning with W, and you have to have gone to Harvard or Boston College to get to the top." On inquiring further, we learned that "a town beginning with a W" meant Weston, Wellesley, or Wayland—all wealthy suburban towns.

"A degree from a prestigious school is as clear a status symbol for class as we have."
—Fred A. Hargadon, Dean of Admissions, Princeton University

We have learned that in many organizations it is important for career advancement to play golf or to sail. In one large conglomerate in Texas, we learned that men who were blond, thin, and handsome were prime candidates for the executive suite. We are told over and over that if your social profile doesn't match that of the senior managers in your organization, your chances of advancement are diminished.

Our Comment

What can you do about this? In terms of yourself, it can be discouraging if everyone above you in the organization looks different from you. But in terms of your direct reports, you have some control. Take another look at who you have hired or promoted. You want to be sure that you yourself do not have an overly rigid prototype for what it takes to be a good manager or supervisor. Be sure that when you evaluate promotability, you are looking at substantive criteria, not superficial qualities.

Often criteria for jobs do not match the real skills needed to do the job well. Educational requirements in particular can eliminate legions of otherwise qualified people from consideration. We have seen this particularly in sales jobs, where there may be strict criteria about having an engineering degree, when actually people with much less education could learn what they needed to know on the job, over time. The effect of this kind of criterion is to keep out candidates with different educational backgrounds and perspectives—in short, to keep out diverse candidates.

Pecking Order Privilege

At a high-tech company in Silicon Valley, there is an annual summer outing to a beautiful ranch. The assemblers, shipping department, and support staff do not get invited. This outing is only for managers and professionals.

We've heard hundreds of versions of this story—the exclusive dining room for executives and the large cafeteria for everybody else; the lawyers who received free baseball tickets, while the paralegals and support staff had to pay; the outing to the boat races where the doctors got free tickets for the grandstand, while the rest of the staff sat on the river bank; the holiday parties for the managers held at fancy restaurants, while those for the union take place in a rented hall. We've even heard of a law firm where the lawyers get free Cokes and everyone else has to use the Pepsi machine. Support staff told us it was deliberately Pepsi so that the lawyers could be sure support staff were not pilfering their supply of Cokes!

OUR COMMENT

As a manager and supervisor, this is an area where you should be hyper-sensitive. If you see your company creating unnecessary distinctions, speak up. Counsel against this kind of caste system. Even when the exclusion is unintentional, the effect is significant. Morale and motivation can be seriously affected. It is probably in your organization's best interest to make sure these kinds of situations are avoided. Managers often perceive these as trivial issues, but when you are in the groups that feel like second-class citizens, it can seem like a major issue.

WORKING EXAMPLES
DISRESPECT

Marlene McLean was hired by an HMO as a receptionist. She was pleased to get the job, but this soon changed. She told us that the atmosphere at the HMO was chaotic and that the doctors were rude. One called her an airhead because she lost several phone calls as she tried to transfer them. She heard another doctor swear at a nurse. That was enough for her, and she quit after the first day.

OUR COMMENT

In some organizations, a climate of disrespect prevails. More often than not, it is the professionals and the senior managers, those at the top, who are rude and disrespectful to employees below them in the pecking order. A surprising number of organizations have cultures that tolerate this kind of abuse—and what is more shocking is that no one dares to step in and deal with the situation.

We urge you to speak up when you hear disrespectful language, especially when it comes from those who are higher up in the organizational hierarchy. It is usually impossible for those low in the pecking order to deal with a rude person who is in a position of authority. It may be very hard for you to blow the whistle, but we encourage you to do it. Here are a couple of comments that you can use in almost every situation: "That sounded rude to me." "Your last comment appears to me to be disrespectful." "Let's not name-call here; it bothers me to hear that." Organizational courage is what is called for.

"Sometimes to be silent is to lie."
—MIGUEL UNAMUNO

STYLE VERSUS SUBSTANCE

Sylvia LeBlanc is an accounts receivable supervisor in a shoe factory. She is hoping to get promoted to the job of comptroller, which has recently opened up. The director of the finance department has told the company president that he doesn't think Sylvia can be given the job. He explains that her skirts are too short, her makeup too heavy, and her necklines too plunging. She just doesn't look like a comptroller.

OUR COMMENT

The director of finance is looking at the wrong set of criteria. He should attend to Sylvia's ability to do the job and her present job performance, not her clothes and personal appearance. If Sylvia isn't violating a company dress code, the director of finance is skating on thin ice on this one. If she is professionally strong, we suggest that he appoint Sylvia to the job. Then he could consider providing her with some counsel about professional dress. This kind of feedback is tricky to give, however, and has the potential to backfire. If there is a dress code, you will have an easier time in handling the situation.

CASTE AT WORK

On the supertankers used by an oil shipping company, there is a sharp separation between the officers and the seamen. There are two dining rooms, two lounges, and two separate sleeping areas, reflecting age-old maritime traditions. This two-caste system means that there is very little informal communication between the two groups, and close relationships across groups are minimal. The seamen rarely offer suggestions to the officers on how the work could be done better.

OUR COMMENT

This is an extreme example of hierarchy in the work setting that demonstrates the downside of rigid distinctions between groups. Not only can caste systems stifle innovation, they can limit all communication. Important issues may go unreported. Some people believe that morale also suffers when you work in this kind of two-class system. Most oil companies today are beginning to question the benefit of their traditional way of working.

We think this questioning process is useful in every work setting. Wherever there are perks, privileges, and distinctions between groups, it is useful to ask whether they are helping the work get done better.

QUESTIONS AND ANSWERS

Q: At the company where I work, we laugh because it is always people who went to Stanford or Berkeley who are promoted. To tell the truth, I really don't think it's all that funny—I went to a state college in Montana, and I resent these rich kids moving along so fast while I'm working long hours and no one is noticing. I can't really say anything, can I?

A: Complaining about this will probably get you nowhere. Networks based on schooling can be real assets to people who went to the right school. If you didn't, of course, it can feel very unfair. What you can do is ask about the specific criteria for promotion and talk with your boss about what you need to do to get promoted. There may be other ways for you to gain access to senior managers, such as serving on a task force or a temporary assignment.

Q: I am a woman who is considered to be a "high-potential" manager in my company. I do not play golf, but I have been told that if I really want to get ahead, I should take it up. What do you think?

A: If golf would be fun for you, we suggest you take some lessons. But if you are only doing it for show, it probably isn't worth it, since it takes a long time and a lot of effort to become proficient. See if you can devise other ways to have social and informal contact with senior managers. How about tennis? One manager we knew made fabulous contacts in his company by volunteering to take a leadership role in the United Way campaign. The bottom line is that there are usually a number of ways to reach the top, and there is no single path to get there.

Q: In my company we had a management training program for middle managers. What happened was that the course turned into a major gripe session. We shared our complaints and frustrations about the lousy job the senior managers are doing. (The company has been losing money for the last year.) We asked to have a session to give the executives some feedback, but it didn't happen. They said they already knew what all the problems are and they were too busy.

A: In our experience, this situation is all too common. Senior managers think they understand what all the issues and concerns are. In actual fact, they may be missing pieces of important information known by those below them in the organization. This is why communication across levels is so critical. We suggest you try again for a meeting. You have a better chance of success if you ask them as a group of managers. Good luck!

Q: Our not-for-profit agency deals with our community's poorest citizens and their most basic needs, such as food and emergency shelter. This year our annual awards banquet was considerably more upscale than ever before—it was held at a ritzy hotel, and the invitation read "black tie optional" and the whole thing felt all wrong to me and some of my colleagues. Our board of trustees is touting the event as a huge success. I'd like to see next year's banquet return to our earlier, more down-to-earth approach. Do I dare make this suggestion?

A: It sounds as if several things may be going on here. Do you believe that too much money was spent on this year's event? Did its tone seem inappropriate in light of the work that your agency does? If, for example, several board members absorbed the additional costs from their own pockets, and the purpose of the enhanced event was to demonstrate the board's support and appreciation of the agency staff, the enhancement might be viewed as relatively benign. This might not be the case if operating budgets had to be cut back because of the extra costs of the event. The key here is to find out what the story is. If your discomfort is more on a personal level—that is, if you don't feel comfortable in "society" settings—perhaps you could suggest changing the nature and venue of the event each year, so that the needs and preferences of various agency constituencies could be addressed at least periodically.

Q: One of the food service workers at our plant recently applied for a receptionist position in my department. I have always found Freida to be pleasant and outgoing—and this new position would be a nice step up for her careerwise. I think she'd be a great fit except for one thing: her teeth. We don't require a beauty queen for this job, but Freida's teeth are distractingly terrible—several are missing, and the ones that are there are discolored and poorly positioned. Our benefits package includes both dental and orthodontal insurance; there's almost no need for anyone to have this problem. Would it be okay to tie her promotion to a promise to do something about her teeth?

A: Your heart is in the right place, however, you're treading in sensitive territory here—legally and interpersonally. Certainly you are entitled to discuss with your receptionist—or candidates for the position—your expectations regarding professional demeanor and appearance in this role. Meeting certain standards in these areas is a job requirement, and a bona fide subject for discussion. However, only bona fide occupational criteria may be used to screen candidates out or in. With regard to Freida's teeth, you might want to discuss her dental appearance in the context of covering all-around appearance and its importance in this job. Try to make it clear that you are rooting for her and want to give her as much of a leg up as possible. But tying promotion to her agreement to dental work is going too far.

Q: Our new switchboard operator is a great person, bubbly and enthusiastic. However, she only recently relocated to our area and her roots are pure New York—and so is her accent. Actually, I think it is what is commonly known as a Brooklyn accent—lots of "dese" and "dose" and a sort of nasal twang to everything. We're a Chicago-based, high-end financial services company with a fairly conservative, well-to-do, midwestern clientele. I'm concerned that when our customers call, the first voice they hear doesn't really fit our image. (A few of them have actually commented on how "low class" she sounds.) How do you suggest we handle this?

A: We've seen a number of cases in which accents, pronunciation, or other such factors have made it difficult for customers or clients to understand what an employee is saying; you have a variation on this fundamental dilemma. What the receptionist says and how she delivers her message—

from tone to volume—certainly does reflect substantially on the company's image. We think you need to do two things here. First, level with your receptionist, and tell her that her accent is a problem. Assure her that the criticism isn't personal, just regional, and that it's important that your organization's presentation support its image as a Midwest-founded, "heartland" organization. Second, if at all possible, offer to help her solve the problem by providing assistance so that she can improve her speech. There are speech coaches, elocution specialists, and even people who specialize in eradicating accents who can help her.

Q: I'm an account manager at an advertising agency. I am supported by a young man who is innately bright and very hardworking and who seems to have a natural flair for our business. I have taken him under my wing and am trying to bring him along professionally, coaching him about his career prospects and taking him to meetings with higher-ups to enhance his visibility. Last month Bob asked if he could tag along to my next session with a particularly important client. So I brought him to yesterday's lunch meeting, which was held at a fancy downtown club to which the client belongs. I was shocked when the meal arrived and he displayed the worst table manners I have ever seen. He never picked up his napkin (let alone putting it on his lap), chewed with his mouth open, speared huge hunks of food, which he then chomped off of the fork, and so on. I was appalled—but worse, I could see from the expression on our client's face that he was noting every nuance of this performance as well. Help!

A: It sounds as if you are doing a fine job of mentoring this young man. Social graces, from appropriate business manners to table etiquette, are not passed from one individual to another via genetics; it's all learned behavior. You need to offer Bob instruction in these skill areas, just as he may require additional training in copywriting or using the new phone system. But raising the subject with him will require much tact and sensitivity on your part. If he resists your offer, back off.

Q: Our company is so hierarchical that we even have separate bathrooms for the professional staff and the support personnel. What can I do?

A: Differentiated benefits have long irked underlings. Some benefits, such as club memberships or stock options, are relatively private, and those who are not accorded them sometimes are not even fully aware of their existence or magnitude. Other "perks" are highly visible and can cause a lot of disgruntlement among the unentitled. Unfortunately, there is not much that can be done about this; only those benefits that are specifically covered by law must be doled out equally. It might be worth pointing out, though, that company loyalty and morale might be well served, at a relatively low cost, by reexamining the bathroom policy.

Q: My boss takes two-hour lunches but holds me, his secretary, to forty-five minutes. I think this is unfair. Is it?

A: We don't think so. The schedule your boss is able to keep is more flexible than yours, but it has its own drawbacks. Most managers end up working between forty-five and sixty hours, and many put in time at home during evenings and weekends. As we see it, the downside of your job is a fixed lunch hour.

ACTION STEPS THAT WORK

1. Be sure company-sponsored social events are as inclusive as possible.
2. Take a look at perks and privileges in your work unit. Ask people about their impact.
3. Sit down with your direct reports and have a conversation about their careers. Ask them about their hopes and aspirations, and help them plan their next steps.
4. Provide a time for employees below you in the hierarchy to offer suggestions about how to do the work better.
5. Ask people in your workgroup, "What are the two or three stupidest things I have done in the last year?" You may be amazed at what you learn.

CREATING COMPETITIVE ADVANTAGE

Do's

- Do be sure you are using objective criteria when you hire or promote.
- Do ask all staff about their concerns and issues and listen carefully to their answers. Ask specifically if anything seems unfair.
- Do encourage your direct reports to disagree with your ideas. Make it clear that that's what you are seeking—independent thinking.
- Do take a hard look at the privileges of rank in your work environment. See if they help the work get done or actually interfere.

Don'ts

- Don't exclude lower-level employees from major organizational social events.
- Don't make snap judgments about people's competence based on superficial matters of style or dress.
- Don't limit your sources for candidates for your applicant pools to a few traditional colleges.
- Don't be afraid to mix several levels of employees on task forces or committees. It's good for everyone.

RESOURCES

ORGANIZATIONS

A.K. Rice Institute, 1600 New Hampshire Ave., N.W., Washington, DC 20029; (202) 328-8805. This organization sponsors workshops examining issues of authority in organizations.

BOOKS

Robert Christopher, *Crashing the Gates: The De-WASPing of America's Power Elite*, New York: Simon & Schuster, 1989.

Benjamin DeMott, *The Imperial Middle: Why Americans Can't Think Straight about Class*, New York: Morrow, 1990.

Barry Oshry, *Power and Position*, Boston: Power and Systems, Inc., 1977.

ARTICLES

"Class in America," *Fortune*, February 7, 1994, pp. 114–125.

"How Much Does Class Matter?" *Fortune*, July 30, 1990, pp. 123–128.

AUDIOVISUALS

The Tale of O., On Being Different in an Organization, Goodmeasure, Cambridge, MA 02139; (617) 621-3838.

"*A Class Divided*," *Frontline*, A PBS Video, 4370 Braddock Pt., Alexandria, VA; 22314; (703) 739-5000 or (800) 344-3337.

CHAPTER 8

GAYS, LESBIANS, AND BISEXUALS—SEXUAL ORIENTATION

ON October 17, 1990, Dan Miller was terminated from his job as a management consultant. Miller had appeared on TV urging more police protection for gays and lesbians and had been identified as "Daniel Miller, Gay Rights Activist." Six weeks later, Miller opened his own consulting office in nearby Harrisburg, Pennsylvania. Some of his clients who chose to go with him received a letter from Dan's former boss saying, in part, "It's well known that homosexuals are significantly at risk for AIDS. While I have no knowledge of Dan's medical condition, consider getting the results of a blood test from him if you are considering using his services on a long-term basis."[1] Far from winning a discrimination suit, Miller was sued by his boss for breach of contract, specifically breach of a noncompetition prohibition. The former employer was awarded $126,648.

Elsewhere in the country, a man named Jeff Collins filed a discrimination suit against Shell Oil and some of its subsidiaries. After nineteen years of employment with Shell, he was fired when an invitation to a gay "safe sex" party he had left in the photocopy room was found. Under a state labor law, he won a record $5.3 million in damages in 1993.

As these two vignettes suggest, one of the most controversial components of diversity is sexual orientation, which may be heterosexual, bisexual, or homosexual. For the purposes of brevity, we use the terms *gay* and *lesbian* to refer to nonheterosexuals throughout this chapter.

As an aspect of diversity, sexual orientation, like religion, may be invisible. People make assumptions about who is gay and who is straight, usually based on stereotypes about behavior, and these

---

[1] James B. Stewart, *The New Yorker*, June 13, 1994, p. 74.

assumptions can be wrong. Individuals actually have no way of ascertaining the sexual orientation of a fellow worker unless that person elects to reveal this information. Most workplaces have policies and a work culture that were shaped when the workforce was mostly white and male. Similarly, most workplaces still assume that their employees are heterosexual.

> "If Lesbians were purple, none would be admitted to respected places. But, if all Lesbians suddenly turned purple today, society would be surprised at the number of purple people in high places."
> —SIDNEY ABBOTT AND BARBARA LOVE, *SAPPHO WAS A RIGHT-ON WOMAN*

Some people are made acutely uncomfortable when they learn that another person is homosexual, while for others it is no big deal, simply part of the way things are. According to a 1992 poll published by *Newsweek*, 80 percent of the population believes that homosexuals should have equal rights in job opportunities. (See Figure 8.1.) Furthermore, Americans are more likely to support equal protection initiatives when they know someone who is gay or lesbian. Unfortunately, most Americans, particularly males, say they don't know anyone who is gay. However, most estimates of the proportion of homosexuals in the overall population range from one in ten to one in twenty. If you have a workplace of more than a dozen people, you may want to reconsider your contention that you don't know anyone who is gay. You probably do.

Even in the mid-nineties, at many Fortune 500 companies the words homosexual, gay, and lesbian are rarely part of formal communication. Many people who accept other kinds of diversity, such as

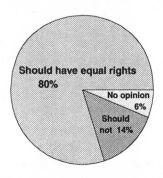

Fig. 8.1 "In general, do you think homosexuals should or should not have equal rights in terms of job opportunities?"
Source: Gallup Poll Questions, 1993.

race or ethnicity, have trouble with sexual orientation. Some people are convinced that sexual orientation is a matter of morality and choice, despite mounting evidence that sexual preference may be determined at least in part by genetic makeup. Homophobia, or strong feelings of fear, dislike, or disgust toward homosexuals, also continues to persist in our culture. In Massachusetts, for example, hate crimes against homosexuals have risen 53 percent in the past three years.

While social exclusion and the glass ceiling are always of concern to homosexuals, the bottom line for most gays and lesbians in the workplace is the distinct possibility of job loss. They report living in constant fear of being found out. Traditionally, most gay men and lesbians in the workplace have had two choices: stay in the closet or face a stalled career and almost certain discrimination. Since the emergence of AIDS in the early eighties, paranoia about the disease has led some people to try to avoid all interaction with homosexuals. But the last decade has also witnessed the emergence of gay pride. There have been gay pride marches in many cities that attract large crowds of gays and lesbians as well as large numbers of straight supporters.

Moreover, as a December 16, 1991, *Fortune* magazine article puts it, "Homosexuality, once a career-destroying secret, is coming out of the closet in corporate America." Groups and associations of gay and lesbian employees meet at a host of companies, including AT&T, Xerox, Boeing, Coors, DuPont, Lockheed, US WEST, Levi Strauss, Apple, and Digital. At many other companies, gay men and lesbians get together unofficially. Professional organizations have also mushroomed in larger cities across the land. In New York City, for example, there are groups for gay men and lesbians in advertising, manufacturing, and publishing, as well as lawyers', physicians', and bankers' groups. Gay men's choruses are sprouting in many cities. The Gay Olympics of 1994 received significant media attention, with over 11,000 athletes from around the world participating.

While it may seem that we've come a long way toward minimizing stereotyping and prejudice based upon sexual orientation, attitudes still vary widely according to geographic location and industry type. In some environments, particularly arts organizations (from advertising agencies to symphony orchestras), there may be acceptance of nonheterosexual orientations. In some parts of the country—San Francisco, for instance, which has long been a center for gays—employers, ranging from local government to private companies, typically exhibit a considerable degree of openness and acceptance. In other areas—such as the Bible Belt—being gay or lesbian may be considered a sin by some people, and organizations may make it clear that those who are openly homosexual are not welcome.

Incidents of homophobia, however, are not limited to conservative religious communities. In 1987, 88 percent of gay or lesbian faculty who responded to a survey conducted at the University of Illinois at Urbana-Champaign believed that being open about their sexual orientation would negatively affect their chances for advancement; 40 percent reported actually being penalized for their orientation in a work situation. In a survey conducted at Oberlin College in 1990, one in eight gay employees reported having been the target of "nonviolent forms of discrimination," including exclusion from social events, lack of promotion, and outright threats and insults. And stereotypes about sexual orientation persist. In the late 1980s, a survey asked respondents to indicate what jobs they believed were most interesting to lesbian women compared to straight women. The results were discouragingly stereotyped. Lesbians were seen to prefer working as auto mechanics, plumbers, or truck drivers, while heterosexual women were perceived to be drawn to interior decorating and nursing.

Individual companies can also differ greatly in how they view the issue of sexual orientation. At a few companies, like Lotus in Cambridge, Massachusetts, a number of people are out of the closet. At other companies, such as a large bank in Utah, even saying the words *gay* and *lesbian* is ground-breaking. During our training sessions, gays and lesbians frequently come up to us at the breaks and thank us profusely for bringing up the issue.

THE LAW

There is no federal legislation protecting gays and lesbians from discrimination in the workplace. In several states there have been attempts to pass laws protecting gays and lesbians, but this has evoked significant opposition. In 1993, the rancorous debate about the role of gays in the military revealed the lack of any broad national consensus about this issue.

Several cities, however, including New York, Washington, D.C., and Philadelphia, have ordinances protecting gays and lesbians, and eight states have passed statutes outlawing employment discrimination against gays and lesbians. (See Figure 8.2.) Proposed federal leg-

▪ California	▪ Minnesota
▪ Connecticut	▪ New Jersey
▪ Hawaii	▪ Vermont
▪ Massachusetts	▪ Wisconsin

Fig. 8.2 States that Include Sexual Orientation in Their Employment Protection Policies
Source: Brian McNaught, *Gay Issues in the Workplace,* New York: St. Martin's Press, 1994

islation to protect gays and lesbians is seen as unlikely to pass in the near future, and recently there have been several heated campaigns attempting to roll back those city and state laws that do offer protection to gays and lesbians.

"Where sexual proclivity does not relate to job function, it seems clearly unconstitutional to penalize an individual in one of the most imperative of life's endeavors, the right to earn one's daily bread."
—SIDNEY H. ASCH, JUDGE, NEW YORK STATE SUPREME COURT, APPELLATE DIVISION

COMMON ISSUES AND CONCERNS
In our work in hundreds of companies in the last five years, four major issues and concerns of gays and lesbians have been consistently brought to our attention.

TO TELL OR NOT TO TELL?
The open, free-wheeling way in which many modern-day Americans share their most intimate secrets—the "I've got nothing to hide" style predominant in many workplaces—presents continual decision points for those with a homosexual orientation. "So what did you do Saturday night?" might seem like innocuous Monday morning chatter, but for a gay man who spent Saturday night at a gay film festival or with a male lover, it requires a decision regarding how truthful one wishes (or can afford) to be. These situations are often perceived by nonheterosexuals as lose-lose scenarios. "If I tell them I was with my lover at a bar," explains one lesbian who lives in Tennessee, "they'll be envisioning me all week in the arms of some tattooed bull-dyke, and most of them will probably decide I don't have much potential in the friend department. On the other hand, if I ignore the question, they'll write me off as stand-offish and snobby. And then nobody will talk to me for sure!"

OUR COMMENT

There are no easy answers for these dilemmas. Individuals need to assess the potential impact on their lives and careers of "coming out" in their organizations and weigh this against the freedom from a life of deception and secrecy. Managers may wish to make this assessment as well, and, following this analysis, do all they can to create a work environment and climate that is supportive of all of the employees in their workgroups.

SOCIAL OCCASIONS/PARTY TIME

Some clients need to be taken to dinner, and most companies have a holiday party or an annual family picnic. These sorts of situations are highly problematic for gay or lesbian individuals who do not wish to reveal their status. Some resort to a "cover" escort (an opposite-sex friend or acquaintance who poses as a significant other); others go it alone and fend off the intrusive questions and well-meaning offers, such as "Don't you have a boyfriend?" or "Can I set you up with my cousin?"

OUR COMMENT

The most important thing for managers and supervisors is to be aware that workers may be gay or lesbian. Being sensitive to this possibility means being careful about all communications and maintaining respect for gays and lesbians, even when you are fairly sure everyone in the group is heterosexual. For example, the invitation below gets bad marks as possibly being offensive to three groups: homosexuals, non-Christians, and singles.

> *Atlas Company invites you and your spouse to its annual Christmas party on December 11 at 7:00 p.m. We hope you can come.*

A better and more sensitive version might read:

> *Atlas Company invites you to the annual Holiday Party on December 11 at 7:00 p.m. We hope you can come. Bring a friend, spouse, or significant other if you'd like.*

With regard to social events, you need to be aware that many of your employees may not be part of traditional families. Let them take the lead in the degree to which they share information about their personal circumstances and respect both candor about their personal circumstances and lack of disclosure.

DISRESPECTFUL LANGUAGE

The most frequently mentioned problem confronting gay and lesbian workers in the workplace is demeaning and disrespectful language about homosexuals: "Look at that fag." "How effeminate can you get?" "What a waste; Mary's a lesbian." Homophobic jokes may be considered acceptable and often provoke almost universal laughter. They are commonplace even in workgroups where employees would not tolerate a racial slur.

OUR COMMENT

It is part of your job to banish jokes and disrespectful language about sexual orientation from your workgroup. Employees will probably need to be educated about this. You need to be clear about which kinds of words are out of bounds. Since sexual orientation is typically invisible, employees may be unknowingly insulting someone in the workgroup, and they need to have their consciousness raised about this possibility.

Sometimes there is deep hurt. For example, the Boston Knights of Columbus, long known for its St. Patrick's Day parade in South Boston, decided to cancel the parade rather than obey a court order allowing gays and lesbians to march. At a bank in that neighborhood, a teller who is a lesbian reported to us that she was startled and upset to hear the comments several customers made about that decision. She said, "I heard people I'd known all my life spouting off profanities about people like me—they didn't even know it. I'm going to have a tough time looking them straight in the eye and smiling the next time they come into the bank. I was thinking about coming out at work," she continued, "but when I think about how everyone here supported those guys... I just don't know."

Homophobia is all too common. As a manager, it is not an easy matter to change attitudes about sexual orientation. What you can do is insist on a work environment free of put-downs, slurs, and disrespect.

"One way I can make the world a better place is to help people understand that there's nothing to be afraid of from lesbians and gays."
—EASTWICK TOR TAYLOR, BAY AREA CAREER WOMEN

BENEFITS FOR GAY MEN AND LESBIANS

In 1991, Lotus Development Corporation announced that it would offer the long-term partners of its homosexual employees the same benefits as the husbands and wives of heterosexuals. Since that announcement, which received extensive media coverage, there has been growing pressure for these benefits in many other organizations. A number of organizations have begun to consider the issue, and many are developing procedures to ensure that same-sex couples to whom benefits would be offered are in long-term relationships. (See Figure 8.3.) Most workplaces at this point in time, however, stop short of offering health-care and other benefits to the partners of gays and lesbians.

OUR COMMENT

Managers and supervisors need to learn about present thinking and existing policies toward gays and lesbians at their organizations. You need to get the facts, but even more importantly, you'll want to feel comfortable explaining your company's position to your people. They may seek advice from you on how to get the organization to extend its benefits. (See Figure 8.4.)

WORKING EXAMPLES
"I WISH I'D SAID SOMETHING"

The human resources department of a rural North Dakota health center has twelve employees, all women, including the unit's manager. The weekly department staff meetings can get a bit rowdy. It is not unusual to hear sexual innuendoes or quips—usually with men as the butt of the humor. At one staff meeting, Rosie recounted a slightly off-color joke; the punchline was a slur on lesbians. Most of the women giggled, but the manager noted that two of the team members were exchanging glances.

The manager said later on, "I wish I'd said something. I knew I should, and I wanted to, but I didn't know what to say. I don't know if Doris and Linda [the two employees who exchanged looks] are lesbians—and, if they are, I'm not sure if anyone else in the department knows. I didn't want to put the spotlight on them, but I couldn't figure out how to respond without doing that."

1 The two parties have resided together for at least six months and intend to do so indefinitely.

2 The two parties are not married, are at least eighteen years old, are not related by blood closer than would bar marriage in California, and are mentally competent to consent to the contract.

3 The two parties declare that they are each other's sole domestic partner and they are responsible for common welfare.

4 The two parties agree to notify the employer if there is any change in the circumstances attested to in the affidavit.

5 The two parties affirm, under penalty of perjury, that the assertions in the affidavit are true to the best of their knowledge.

1. A specific employment policy that prohibits discrimination based on sexual orientation

2. Creation of a safe work environment that is free of heterosexist, homophobic, and AIDSphobic behaviors

3. Companywide education about gay issues in the workplace and about AIDS

4. An equitable benefits program that recognizes the domestic partners of gay, lesbian, and bisexual employees

5. Support of gay/lesbian/bisexual employee support group

6. Freedom for all employees to participate fully in all aspects of corporate life

7. Public support of gay issues

Fig. 8.3 Spousal Equivalent Benefits
Source: Brian McNaught, *Gay Issues in the Workplace*, New York: St. Martin's Press, 1994

Fig. 8.4 What Gay, Lesbian, and Bisexual Employees Want at Work
Source: Brian McNaught, *Gay Issues in the Workplace*, New York: St. Martin's Press, 1994

OUR COMMENT

This manager could have intervened and protected everyone's privacy by focusing on the issue, not the particular people who might be offended. It would have been reasonable for the manager to say, "That comment is really unacceptable here. In this workgroup I don't want anyone put down, including lesbians—or men either, for that matter!"

This example underscores the point made earlier: It is hard to set limits on jokes, but it is part of the manager's job. It's what you get paid to do. And it's never too late to begin. Even if you have let these kinds of comments go by for years, it's okay to change. You can even make a joke on yourself and say something about recently seeing the light, etc.

AT RISK OF TERMINATION

Cheryl Summerville was fired in 1991 from a Cracker Barrel restaurant in Georgia. This resulted from the chain's sudden announcement that it would no longer employ individuals "whose sexual preferences fail to demonstrate normal heterosexual values." Because this occurred in a state with no antidiscrimination laws on the books, Summerville had no legal recourse.

OUR COMMENT

As this vignette reveals, the risk of losing your job if you are identified as gay or lesbian is still real in the workplace of the 1990s. Prejudice against gays and lesbians is particularly difficult to change, partly because it is so often coupled with religious or moral values. Therefore, we are typically very hesitant about telling anyone to come out of the closet. But there are also risks, as one of this chapter's opening vignettes demonstrates, for the organization that behaves shabbily toward homosexuals. At this point in time, geography makes the difference: only eight states and 110 municipalities have statutes barring discrimination against gays. Many individual companies, however, have policies stating that they will not discriminate on the basis of sexual orientation. (See Figure 8.5.)

GAY PRIDE

Murray, who is an energetic software engineer in a high-tech company in Silicon Valley, is not out of the closet. However, he is organizing a fund-raiser for AIDS and has been soliciting people for the fundraiser in the cafeteria. His picture also appeared in the local newspaper at the head of a Gay Pride parade wearing a T-shirt with the company name on it. His manager hasn't spoken to him about any of these activities.

OUR COMMENT

We don't think there is any need to talk to Murray. However, if a manager or supervisor is supportive, he or she can show it by actions such as contributing to the AIDS fund-raiser, attending the fund-raiser, or marching in a Gay Pride parade. This scenario illustrates the complexity that often accompanies these situations. Some of Murray's behaviors—soliciting in the cafeteria, for instance—may violate company policy. The manager should deal with any such violations sensitively, but firmly.

What Murray does on his own time—leading a Gay Pride parade, for example—is not appropriate grounds for official action. If, however, the photograph featuring Murray in this role wearing a company T-shirt has caused concern at the company, Murray's manager may need to take action on this point. To identify the best course in this sticky scenario, we advise Murray's supervisor to consult with his or her manager and the human resources department. In sum, there may be legitimate organizational concerns here; it is critical, however, that Murray be dealt with fairly and with dignity.

▪ Disney World	▪ US WEST
▪ AT&T	▪ Kodak
▪ Xerox	▪ 3M
▪ Digital	▪ Bellcore
▪ Chase Manhattan Bank	▪ Procter & Gamble

Fig. 8.5 Some of the Companies with Policies against Discrimination on the Basis of Sexual Orientation
Source: Brian McNaught, Gay Issues in the Workplace, New York: St. Martin's Press, 1994

QUESTIONS AND ANSWERS

Q: Tad, a young man in my workgroup, has told me he is gay. He has asked me whether he should tell his coworkers he is gay or stay in the closet. I think it could hurt his career to come out. Should I tell him that?

A: Giving advice on this probably doesn't make sense. Give him your general support, but avoid specific suggestions as to what he should do. Help him consider the pros and cons of both alternatives.

Q: I am definitely a supporter of nondiscrimination for gays and lesbians. What changes would gays and lesbians like to see in the workplace?

A: Most gays and lesbians would like to feel that they will not face a hostile work environment because of their sexual orientation. They look forward to the day when it will be safe to come out of the closet. Many also want health-care benefits for spousal equivalents.

Q: I'm on a new diversity council in my company. One member of the council, Vivienne, has recently come out as a lesbian within the council, but not at large. She urges us to make health insurance coverage for same-sex partners our number one priority. I'm concerned that starting our diversity work with this issue might not be the political thing to do. What shall I do?

A: Part of your effectiveness as a manager is in judging when an organization is ready for major changes such as the one

Vivienne has proposed. Since your diversity council is still new, you may need to establish credibility by accomplishing something else first. On the other hand, if you test the waters, you may discover that this is a very appropriate issue for the group. Use your own best judgment, but sit down with Vivienne and explain your conclusions to her.

Q: My boss is pretty ignorant regarding gays, lesbians, and bisexuals. Is there a book you could suggest to help him get more knowledgeable?

A: Until recently the pickings in this area were slim, but finally there are several good books out, including one by Brian McNaught in our resource list. Check the resource list at the end of this chapter as well as references to articles that could educate your boss. We think it's a good idea to offer a book or article to him.

Q: My company just never addresses these issues at all! How can I encourage my organization to "get with it" without coming out myself?

A: You might try going in confidence to the human resources person you trust the most and discussing this with her or him. You might suggest a film on the topic or an article that could be passed around.

Q: My company has denied same-sex partner benefits on the basis of cost, stating that if they gave them to gays, all live-ins would demand them. I don't feel that this is fair, and I'd like to see the issue reconsidered. What's the best strategy here?

A: Many organizations have recently undertaken consideration same-sex partner benefits with mostly positive outcomes. It might be helpful for you to research this phenomenon a bit, locate a company (Lotus, for example) that has decided to move in this direction, and use that company as a model and a resource. Contact the benefits manager and find out how that company responded to the "equity" argument. Also, see if you can get copies of the literature it put out about the new benefit—the language and style of presentation may help you generate suggestions for approaches your own company could take.

Q: I'm a twenty-six-year-old, about-to-be-married female staff assistant who works for the director of operations at a hospital. My boss is a militant lesbian who continually makes anti-male comments that make me both uncomfortable and angry. Should I speak up, or just keep my thoughts to myself?

A: We feel that comments against any group are inappropriate at work. It wouldn't matter if your boss targeted the elderly, a racial group, or any other population. The next time she makes such a remark, you need to confront her. It can be tough, we know, to do this with one's boss; to make the conversation easier, be certain to stick to what is bothering you, namely the anti-male comments. You can say to her something as simple as, "I feel uncomfortable with that comment."

Q: One man in my workgroup openly describes himself as bisexual. I'm confused—what does this mean, exactly?

A: A bisexual is a person who is open to sexual relationships with persons of either sex. For more on the subject, take a look at the video, "Gay Issues in the Workplace: Gay, Lesbian, and Bisexual," in which these employees speak for themselves. It is listed in the resources section at the end of the chapter.

Q: I'm the manager of a small real estate office, and I have recently become aware that two of my brokers have begun a romantic relationship. This is complicated by the fact that they are both women (I'm a male). They have asked to have the same days off. This messes up my scheduling. What should I do? Should I acknowledge their relationship?

A: The real question here is whether this relationship is interfering with the work of the office. It sounds as if their request is a problem, and you should feel free to deny it. But it doesn't sound as if there is any reason to talk about their personal relationship or to acknowledge it.

ACTION STEPS THAT WORK

1. Read an article (see the resource list) to learn more about gays and lesbians.
2. Pass out reading materials to your workgroup to increase their awareness of the issue.
3. Announce to your workgroup that you value diversity of all kinds; and mention specifically race, gender, sexual orientation, ethnicity, religion, and age. Just saying the words is helpful.
4. Ask your human resources department about its views on benefits for same-sex partners. Find out if the company is considering this option.
5. Bring in experts to conduct an in-service training program on homophobia for your workgroup.

CREATING COMPETITIVE ADVANTAGE

Do's

- Do try to learn more about issues affecting gays and lesbians.
- Do confront any discrimination against homosexuals that you observe in the workplace.
- Do be respectful of the wide range of perspectives on sexual orientation that people in your workgroup may have.
- Do ask the human resources department if your organization has a policy prohibiting discrimination on the basis of sexual orientation. If not, encourage it to develop one.

Don'ts

- Don't ignore slurs or jokes about homosexuals. Say, "That comment is inappropriate for this work environment."
- Don't make assumptions about who is straight and who is gay. Appearances and observed behavior can be deceptive.
- Don't minimize how difficult it can be for the gay or lesbian employee.
- Don't pass over a candidate for a job because you think he or she may be homosexual. Focus on the candidate's ability to do the job.

RESOURCES

ORGANIZATIONS

American Civil Liberties Union, National Gays and Lesbian Rights Project, 132 West 43rd St., New York, NY 10036; (212) 944-9800, Ext. 545.

National Gay and Lesbian Task Force, 1734 14th St., NW, Washington, DC 20009-4309; (202) 332-6483.

Hollywood Supports, 6430 Sunset Boulevard, Suite 102, Los Angeles, CA 90028; (213) 962-3023.

BOOKS

Don Baker and Sean Strub, *Cracking the Corporate Closet*, New York: HarperCollins, 1993.

Brian McNaught, *Gay Issues in the Workplace*, New York: St. Martin's Press, 1993.

Ed Mickens, *The 100 Best Companies for Gay Men and Lesbians*, New York: Pocket Books, 1994.

ARTICLES

Barbara Presley Noble, "A Quiet Liberation for Gay and Lesbian Employees," *New York Times*, June 13, 1993, Section 3, p. 4.

Louise Sloan, "Do Ask, Do Tell: Lesbians Come Out," *Glamour*, May 1994, p. 242.

Thomas A. Stewart, "Gay in Corporate America," *Fortune*, Dec. 16, 1991, pp. 42–56.

AUDIOVISUALS

Gay Issues in the Workplace: Gay, Lesbian, and Bisexual Employees Speak for Themselves, with Brian McNaught, 1994. TRB Publications, P.O. Box 2342, Boston, MA 02107.

Gender and Sexual Orientation Workplace Issues, part of the Diversity Series. 20 minutes, 1993. Quality Media Resources, 10929 S.E. 23rd Street, Bellevue, WA 98004.

The Power of Diversity: Module VII, Sexual Orientation, CorVision Media, 1359 Barclay Blvd., Buffalo Grove, IL 60089; (800) 537-3130.

CHAPTER 9

PARENTS—WORK AND FAMILY

THE SUBJECT

"I can't believe the guys at work; it's unbelievable the ribbing they are giving me," reports Pete Milosovich. Pete is babysitting two days a week for his infant daughter while his wife, Heidi, returns to her job part-time. Pete reports that the guys at the construction firm where he works call him almost every day. Recently, one guy asked him, "Hey, Pete, are you coming to work tomorrow, or will you be breast-feeding?" The next day another coworker called and commented, "I hope you've got your makeup on."

Fifty years ago, when fewer women worked and the majority of men had wives at home, parenting and caretaking issues were rarely raised at the work site. Care of children and aging relatives was the concern and responsibility of the at-home individual, usually a woman. In fact, many women spent the majority of their adult lives at home taking care of someone, beginning with their children and continuing with the care of others.

That has changed. Today 60 percent of men in the workforce have wives who are also employed. There are more than 30 million dual-career couples, more than half of them with children under eighteen. (See Figure 9.1 and 9.2.) Women now make up 46 percent of the workforce. More than 80 percent of the women who are entering the workforce today will get pregnant during their working lives, and 50 percent of the women who get pregnant will return to work before their child's first birthday. In 1994, three-fourths of the women with school-age children were employed outside the home. But this is not just a parents-with-young-children issue. One study predicts that in the United States by the year 2000, there will be more adults with dependent elders relying on them than with children dependent on them. Another study reports that 40 percent of workers expect to have some responsibility for their aging parents.

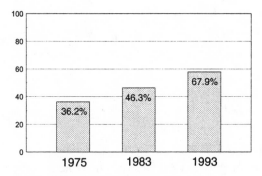

Fig. 9.1 Increase in Percentage of Families where Both Parents Work
  Source: U.S. Bureau of the Census.

Being in the workforce *and* shouldering family responsibilities can cause stress and burnout in individuals. The conflict has a negative impact on the organization as well: When work and family demands conflict, productivity drops. It is clearly in the best interest of organizations to be as helpful as possible.

PIONEERS

Several companies are way out in front in their support of families. (See Figure 9.3.) They have consistently been noted as companies that are family-friendly. Each of them offers slightly different alternatives; each of their programs evolved in a unique way.

Organizations perceived as family-friendly have a far easier time recruiting the employees they want than other organizations. They

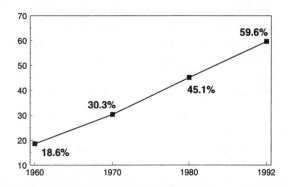

Fig. 9.2 Labor Force Participation Rate of Married Women with Children Under 6 Years
  Source: U.S. Bureau of Labor Statistics.

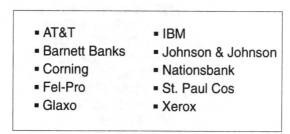

• AT&T • IBM
• Barnett Banks • Johnson & Johnson
• Corning • Nationsbank
• Fel-Pro • St. Paul Cos
• Glaxo • Xerox

Fig. 9.3 Top 10 Family-Friendly Companies
Source: Working Mother Magazine, September 16, 1993.

also have an easier time retaining valued employees. Research demonstrates that employee turnover and absenteeism are reduced when companies have family-supportive policies and practices. However, organizations vary widely in their degree of support for parents and other caregivers. As increasing numbers of organizations are seeing that it is important to provide flexibility for family caregivers, a wide array of flexible work arrangements is becoming part of the workplace scene. One of the major factors in choosing a job is its impact on one's family life. (See Figure 9.4.)

Sometimes managers and supervisors have clear policies and well-accepted organizational practices to guide them in making decisions concerning caretaking issues. In many cases, however, these people face day-to-day judgment calls about how to handle the requests for flexibility that parents and caregivers make. Often there are no policies or consistent practices to guide them in responding to these requests. Many times a decision needs to be made right on the spot. All of this is especially difficult since those who are not parents or caretakers may be watching intently, poised to complain about favoritism.

THE LAW

There is no federal law that prohibits employers from discriminating against parents in the workplace. However, interview or screening questions about marital or parental status are often used to discriminate against women and may violate Title VII of the Civil Rights Act as well as various state antidiscrimination laws. Generally, for a

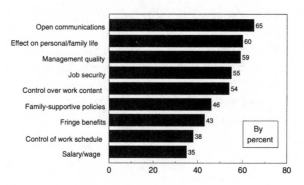

Fig. 9.4 What Today's Employees Want
Factors Considered "Very Important" in the Decision to Take Current Job
Source: Families and Work Institute.

question to be legitimate, it must be job-related. The following questions may constitute direct evidence of discrimination and should be avoided:

"Are you married or planning to get married?"
"Do you have children or are you planning to have children?"
"Will you need to make child care arrangements?"

Although it may seem obvious, even visible signs of pregnancy do not make this a legitimate subject to broach. In 1978, Title VII was amended to prohibit employment discrimination based on "pregnancy, childbirth, or related medical conditions." What this means is that it is unlawful sex discrimination to discriminate against women because they are pregnant. For all employment purposes, employers must treat pregnancy and related conditions the same as they treat other temporary disabilities suffered by employees. Thus, if an employer has a short-term disability policy, it must be made available to employees who are disabled because of pregnancy.

In 1987, the Supreme Court upheld a California law that requires employers to give pregnant women benefits involving unpaid leave and reinstatement—despite the fact that this kind of benefit may not be available to men with temporary disabilities. In addition, many state maternity laws provide that women who return to work after maternity leave must not lose any of the seniority or benefits to which they were entitled before they started their leave.

Where there is no pregnancy-related disability involved, employers cannot adopt policies that afford greater child-rearing benefits to women than to men. For example, it is unlawful sex discrimination for an employer to deny a child-rearing leave to a man when it gives women postmaternity child-rearing leave. The theory is that both men and women are equally capable of child rearing, and it is unfair to grant females preferential treatment.

The Family and Medical Leave Act of 1993 requires that employers with fifty or more employees grant up to twelve weeks of unpaid leave annually to male and female employees for the birth, adoption, or foster care placement of a child, to care for a spouse or an immediate family member with a serious health condition, or when the employee's own serious health condition makes the employee unable to work. During such leaves, employers are required to maintain an employee's existing health coverage at the same level as if the employee were continuously employed. At the end of a leave, employers must reinstate the employee in the same job that the employee held before taking leave or an equivalent job. This federal law differs from some state laws, so be sure to ask the human resources department about your state laws as well.

COMMON ISSUES AND CONCERNS
STRESS AND CONFLICT

For many parents in the workplace, shouldering the responsibility for their children while meeting their job demands can create a crisis from time to time. Some parents are stressed out most of the time. Long hours of work at home caring for children and household can leave some employees so exhausted that their effectiveness is seriously diminished.

Even for the best organized people there will be occasional problems: caregiving systems break down, day care can be closed for a snow day, the sitter gets sick, or an aging parent needs to be taken to the doctor for a series of treatments. All these not-too-out-of-the-ordinary family events can create tension for the employee and headaches for those in management roles.

"It's important to us that people become productive and work. When they're worried about other issues, they're not as productive."
—DIANE CAPSTAFF, JOHN HANCOCK

OUR COMMENT

A supportive supervisor or manager can make a world of difference to a worker facing the minor hassles and serious crises that families entail. Particularly where company policy is essentially ambiguous, it falls on managers and supervisors to figure out the best course of action. In general, the more flexibility you can provide, the better. Studies indicate that it is rare for employees to abuse flexibility. What can be a problem, however, are the perceptions of noncaregiving individuals in the workgroup. They may perceive the flexibility allotted to caretakers as inequitable treatment or favoritism. They may also fear that work that is not accomplished because of the caregiver's flexible hours may fall on them. For these reasons, it is important to manage ongoing flexible work arrangements with the whole workgroup. Bring others into the problem solving whenever possible.

PREGNANCY

Despite the law that precludes treating pregnancy as a unique condition, we believe that pregnancy does raise some special issues that are difficult for supervisors and managers. Do you truly go ahead blindly and hire or promote someone who is seven months pregnant, for example? Pregnant employees will probably require some special flexibility—they may need to come in late or leave early for doctor's appointments, for instance. How far should you go in accommodating pregnancy-related requests?

> "It is still a fundamental fact of life that women have babies and with them, despite the amount of time men dedicate to household chores, a disproportionate responsibility for their care."
> —FELICE SCHWARTZ

OUR COMMENT

As with any situation in which a current employee needs special accommodation, the question for employers is, "Why bother to give it?" There are good business reasons for attempting to meet the needs of workers with family responsibilities, and this includes pregnant women.

First, you have made an investment in this individual. You have trained her; she has a wealth of information and experience specific to her job and your organization. Research studies have clearly demonstrated that replacing an individual under these circumstances results in considerably more cost and dislocation than accommodating her with workplace flexibility

In addition, a recent study shows that pregnant women who saw their workplaces as accommodating while they were pregnant were very appreciative and gave back to their organizations in many different ways.[1] They worked at home while on maternity leave—often at no pay—far more often than others. They returned to work sooner than their colleagues who saw their workplaces as nonaccommodating, and they returned to work at a much higher rate (75 percent, compared to 50 percent of the women in the nonaccommodating organizations). This research is compelling. Thus, we encourage you to be as supportive and flexible as possible with your pregnant workers—knowing that they will give back to you.

The Slow Track—Glass Ceilings and Maternal Walls

Many women tell us that their career is sidetracked once they have a child, and particularly after the birth of a second child. Sometimes they are told outright that they have too many family responsibilities to take on the next-level job. Often it is just assumed that their priorities have shifted and that the job is now second.

> "It appears to be in a company's self-interest to minimize the amount of workplace-family role strain an employee experiences to reduce stress and increase physical and emotional well-being."
> —Bradley Googins and Diana Burden

In our work with companies across the country, several managers told us that employees who leave at five o'clock on the dot are perceived as not serious about their commitment to the organization. At a West Coast utility company we ran into the boss of a woman named Lucia. Lucia left work every day at five to pick up her children at day care. Lucia's boss told us that they probably wouldn't promote her because "she wasn't ambitious."

A great deal has been written about the issue of the "mommy track," or dividing women into those who place their family as their major priority and those who place their job first. More recently the concept of a maternal wall has been set forth—the idea that mothers

---

[1] C.S. Piotrkowski, D. Hughes, J. Pleck, S. Kessler-Skler, G. Stones, "The Experience of Childbearing Women in the Workplace: the impact of family friendly policies and practices." in *Final Report to Women's Bureau*, Washington D.C.: U.S. Department of Labor, 20210.

are seriously blocked in moving forward. Barriers resulting from family circumstances can, of course, be encountered by any employee—male or female—who is perceived to be more concerned about caregiving responsibilities than the workplace culture has traditionally permitted.

"When I went to Harvard Business School, I was told you could have it all—career, marriage, family. No one told me *how* to do it."
—MBA MOM QUOTED BY SWISS AND WALKER.

OUR COMMENT

For employers today, responding to the needs of employees who are also caregivers is not a political issue, it is a practical concern. There are simply too many employees juggling these roles. To ignore their needs would limit one's workforce so dramatically as to impair its quality. Thus, accommodation must be made—not just at the hiring end of the employment process, but throughout the employee's organizational engagement. And, in addition to simple tolerance of the need for flexibility and accommodation, multiple-role employees today (especially women) are also looking to employers to minimize the negative impact of their situation on their career progress.

It is important for managers and supervisors, when they are considering candidates for promotions, for example, to be sure that they aren't making assumptions about employees—particularly those with small children. All you need to know is whether or not an employee can meet the job requirements. Caretaking arrangements, personal values, and family needs vary drastically.

What you may not know is that one woman has virtually fool-proof child care, as her mother lives in her house, whereas another has a fragile childcare system and an unsupportive husband, and is unwilling to travel. Some parents are oriented to the fast track; others may wish for a greater balance between work and family commitments. You can't provide motivation; workers are motivated by their own needs and values.

What managers *can* do, however, is align work circumstances and employee motivation to closely match jobs to employee wishes and needs. For example, many clever managers today are taking advantage of the desires of large numbers of highly skilled, motivated employees to work less than full-time schedules. They are hiring cadres of part-time professional women who prove to be outstandingly productive, reliable, and loyal. Both parties reap the benefits of these innovative arrangements.

MIT professor Lotte Bailyn warns against judging employee competence by the number of hours at work, which she considers "face time," and urges that employees be measured by quality of work. Monitor your preconceptions about hours clocked in and productivity. Many part-time workers are among the most productive we've seen, as they allot little time for socializing, etc. The question is how much work is accomplished, not how many hours people work. If flexibility to work nights and weekends or to travel is key to the job, be sure to explore the employee's ability to respond to these needs; don't assume that the schedule she keeps daily is the only one available to her. She may have shaped her child care arrangements around the requirements of her current job and might alter them if the need arose. The best solution: check it out! (See Figure 9.5.)

> "Time is a proxy indicator for performance, based on some crazy assumption that the more time, the better."
> —LOTTE BAILYN, MIT.

TURNOVER

Child-care dilemmas or demanding family responsibilities may pressure employees to leave a job. In many workplaces, the inflexibility of organizational policy has made it difficult for women to stay on the job and respond adequately to the ebb and flow of needs at home. The typical career pattern for women, as opposed to men, includes mov-

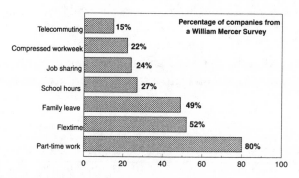

Fig. 9.5 Flexible Work Arrangements: 1990
Source: William M. Mercer, Inc., *Employer Initiatives on Work and Family Issues,* 1991

ing in and out of the workforce during the course of the life cycle. More flexible, accommodating organizational policies could minimize a great deal of this movement. Organizations that are committed to assisting employees in balancing work and family needs will be able to recruit and retain the best of the labor force. If you are aware that it probably costs more to replace a worker than to provide flexibility, your course of action may be easier to figure out.

> "More and more executives are making career decisions based solely on what kind of a home life they can have with a particular job."
> —KATHLEEN CHRISTIANSEN, CITY UNIVERSITY OF NEW YORK.

OUR COMMENT
Sometimes companies are so focused on filling open slots that they neglect to consider what is causing their loss of employees. We find that many managers don't keep track of their turnover rates, so they don't even know how much employee turnover is costing them. It's important to conduct an exit interview so you can get the straight word on why an employee is actually leaving. You will learn—over time—important information about your work environment, and you may discover some ways to retain your competent employees.

FAIRNESS AND FLEXIBILITY—IMPLEMENTING FLEXIBLE WORK ARRANGEMENTS
There are many options in work arrangements that can be used to support employees with children and dependents. You can consider flextime, part-time jobs, school hours, compressed workweeks, job sharing, and telecommuting. Your organization may offer financial assistance with regular childcare, emergency child care, sick child care, elder-care assistance, or resource and referral help. However, many organizations never even consider any of these options. They are operating close to the edge, and they automatically reject any option that has the potential to cost them even a modest sum of money.

OUR COMMENT
Be sure you are aware what your organization offers in the way of flexibility. If you aren't sure, ask the human resources department. Many companies don't announce these options for fear of receiving many requests. This rarely happens, and employees and supervisors should

be fully aware of all the organizational options at their disposal to deal with work and family issues.

As with any benefit, these programs can be either an administrative nightmare or a tool for retaining valuable employees. While we believe that these kinds of benefits are the wave of the future, we recognize that no one of them is appropriate for every situation. We urge you, however, to explore their suitability for your workgroup with an open mind and to consider tailoring them to fit. If at all possible, lean toward flexibility. Remember, the diverse workforce requires a new definition of fairness: Instead of giving everybody the same thing, give everybody what they need. This is a true managerial challenge, but the upside potential for positive impact is enormous.

WORKING EXAMPLES
MISSING PERSONS

Maria works as an assistant to Jerry in a finance department that has recently lost two staff persons because of downsizing. Maria, an average performer, has two small children. When she first started the job six months ago, Maria came in late to work about once a week. More recently, her son has been ill with pneumonia, and she needs to have a sitter come to the house instead of taking him to day care. Arrangements have fallen through on several occasions, and Maria has missed seven days of work in the last three weeks. The rest of the staff is grumbling because they have had to pick up her work when they are already stretched.

OUR COMMENT

This is a typical work and family problem. We feel that Maria deserves some flexibility because the most serious aspect of the problem seems to be time-limited. But we think that Jerry and Maria need to talk on a regular basis. Jerry needs to explain what flexibility he can offer her and what he can't. He must make it clear that this rate of absenteeism can't continue. If possible, he might visit the human resources department prior to this conversation to gain its assistance in generating help for Maria. It may know of sick childcare at a local hospital or of emergency sitting agencies with good track records. If the absenteeism continues, she will have to consider taking a leave or even, perhaps, giving up her job.

BABY AT THE OFFICE

June, who works for a not-for-profit research institute, had a baby two months ago. She has asked her supervisor, Isabel, if she can bring the baby to work for a while. Jane explained that she is nursing and that it would be a problem to be away from the baby for eight hours.

OUR COMMENT

This is the kind of request where all we can say is, "It all depends on the situation." We've seen cases where bringing a baby to work worked out just fine, because there was enough space and privacy for the baby. At other settings, it has been a problem—a colicky baby has wreaked havoc in an otherwise harmonious workgroup. Fairness is another concern. If June can bring her baby to work, clearly other women in the office who are pregnant may assume that it will be fine for them to do the same thing.

Another option is a flexible schedule. This option is being used in places where bringing a baby to work is not viable. Other organizations offer breast pumps, lounge areas, and refrigerator storage space for nursing mothers who return to the job and wish to continue breastfeeding.

DYING DAD

Donald's aging father entered the hospital a few weeks ago. Now Donald, a cutter in a large shoe factory, tells his manager, Rick, that his dad is dying. He wants to take two months off to be with his dad.

OUR COMMENT

This is a no-brainer. Under the new Family Leave and Medical Act, it is Donald's right to have this time off—as long as the company has fifty or more employees. The only issue here is attitudinal. Since Donald is entitled to this option, why not send him off with a supportive "hope all goes as well as possible" rather than a show of irritation at the potential inconveniences his leave taking may prompt? Your support of him in time of need will be remembered and appreciated. Remember also: Emergencies of this kind can happen to *any* employee. Treat others as *you* would like to be treated in similar circumstances.

QUESTIONS AND ANSWERS

Q: I am a manager in a large high-tech company. I have agreed to let two women work at home two days a week. How can I be sure they are actually putting in their hours?

A: You can't. We all need to change the way we measure performance from hours put in—i.e, the aforementioned face time—to performance-based appraisal. Is the work getting done? Does the quantity seem to match the number of hours worked? Is it of good quality? That's what matters.

Q: A woman in my workgroup wants to go to her daughter's school conference during work hours. I feel that if I let her go, everyone will ask me for the same privilege. I plan to say no—what do you think?

A: "It all depends" is the short answer. One variable is the type of work that is done in your organization. Someone managing mutual fund accounts, for example, may need to be at his or her desk all day, every day, in order to do the job. Other types of work allow for more flexibility. We recommend that each workgroup establish a policy and guidelines for taking time away from the work site. These guidelines might be developed by including employees in the discussion. If workers generate suggestions for managing this sort of flexibility fairly, they will be far less likely to complain than if you make a unilateral decision. Lack of consistency is a problem: Just saying "no" in a knee-jerk fashion is also not the wisest course.

Q: I just interviewed a potential secretarial candidate who really impressed me. She seemed sharp, her skills were top-notch, and she appeared to have a pleasant personality. She mentioned in passing, however, that she has three children, all under the age of ten. I didn't raise the issue—I know better than that—but now that I know, I'm a little nervous about hiring her. I need a reliable person. What should I do?

A: Don't prejudge the situation. Assuming that you do a reference check, if her past employers note no problems, go ahead and make the hire—it sounds like you may have hit the jackpot!

Q: I'm a bit miffed. As the mother of two sons, I don't exactly understand all the fuss over Take Your Daughter to Work Day. My employer had special programs for daughters and moms, and even gave them a free luncheon! What about the boys—and their moms?

A: This program got a lot of heat for excluding sons—and, in some quarters, dads. Nonetheless, we think the program is worth defending. Our society still has some distance to go in offering equal opportunities to girls and in encouraging them to consider nonstereotypical career options. We also think that there is a need to support the raising of male children with enlightened views so that ultimately we will have an adult population of males and females who are free of stereotypes. Why not encourage your employer to think in terms of a series of work/family programs that might include a coed program for employees' children?

Q: A woman who works for me wants to continue nursing her child after she returns to work from her maternity leave. She has asked to meet with me to discuss the necessary arrangements. Do I need to—or want to—get into this?

A: This is becoming a not-so-unusual situation as more and more women are continuing to work following the birth of a child. The specifics of the arrangements that will be required will depend on a number of variables, such as where the baby is in child care, the employee's schedule and the nature of her work, and the workplace physical plant. You will need to hear how she envisions making this all work: You might be able to contribute more to solving the problem if you knew more about how other companies have handled this situation. Ask your human resources department to source out the best practices at other organizations so that you can benefit from the work they have done on this issue.

Q: My director of marketing is going through infertility treatments, and it feels as if we are all going through them with her. She's in and out, getting shots and examinations, and seems to be on edge all the time. What gives here, and how should I manage this situation to make the best of it for Donna—and the rest of us?

A: We urge employers to work with employees to attempt to be supportive of all medical processes, including infertility treatments. You may need to meet with Donna periodically to discuss what's ahead for her and what kind of accommodations she'd like. You should also consider what you will need from her to make this all work out satisfactorily from the organization's side. It's a two-way negotiation, and flexibility on all sides usually makes for a win/win solution. Make it work.

Q: Every time it snows, my lab technician brings his kids to work. It seems as if the schools close at the drop of a snowflake, and I'm not sure we can handle the disruption on such a frequent basis. Am I being inflexible?

A: You need to sit down with your assistant and discuss this issue. How much kid time can your lab handle? Perhaps you could define a policy that permits him to bring the kids in a rare emergency, when planning ahead simply is impossible; since we know there will be snow days, advance arrangements could be made to cover this eventuality. Or could he do some work at home on a few of these days? There are probably a number of ways to tackle this problem, but they will all begin by your discussing it together.

Q: I've heard that some companies also offer help in managing problems with older relatives. Is this true?

A: It certainly is. Work/family support encompasses the broad category of dependent care. This obviously includes children, but it also extends to other dependents, such as elderly parents. The categories of assistance are much the same as those for parenting concerns: seminars, information and referral, flexible time-off arrangements to deal with special circumstances, and, occasionally, financial contribution.

Q: I supervise Chuck, an employee whose mother (who lives halfway across the country) had a stroke several months ago. She was recently released from the hospital. I know

Chuck is trying to make good arrangements for her, but in the past few weeks he's missed several important meetings because of crises related to her care. The unpredictability of the situation is making for some tension in our office. What do you suggest?

A: Sit down with Chuck and talk about his situation and your concerns about its impact. This may be a good time for Chuck to travel to where his mother is and take care of making arrangements from nearby, instead of trying to organize her care long distance. This is exactly what the Family Leave Act is for. Explore this and other options together.

ACTION STEPS THAT WORK

1. Hold in-service training sessions; educate workers about caretaking issues and quandaries. Encourage the workgroup to problem-solve about what will work for the group.

2. Familiarize yourself and your employees with the flexible working arrangements available to them as parents. Find out about services such as lunchtime parenting seminars, EAPs, counseling, or an information and referral network.

3. Encourage workers to attend programs on caregiving issues and policies. Familiarize yourself and your employees with the Family and Medical Leave Act and its implications.

4. Meet with other managers and discuss providing flexibility to your workers. Use day-to-day dilemmas you have faced and see if you—as a group—can develop some consistency.

CREATING COMPETITIVE ADVANTAGE

Do's	Don'ts
• Do consider that being fair may mean treating different people differently. • Do encourage men, as well as women, to use the benefits and options available to them. • Do think about flexibility as a business issue, a competitive issue. • Do measure performance on output and quality.	• Don't confuse fairness with consistency and uniformity. • Don't be afraid to try out some experimental arrangements, such as working at home or job sharing. • Don't make assumptions about jobs or promotions based on traditional gender roles or stereotypes about parents. • Don't measure performance on face time, i.e., hours at work. • Don't treat family and parenting problems as women's problems, see them as workplace issues.

RESOURCES

ORGANIZATIONS

The Bureau of National Affairs, 1231 25th St., NW, Washington, DC 20037; (800) 372-1033. *Special Report Series on Work and Family.*

Catalyst, 250 Park Ave South, New York, NY 10003-1459; (212) 777-8900.

Work-Family Directions, 930 Commonwealth Avenue, West, Boston, MA 02215-1274; (617) 278-4000.

The Partnership Group, Inc., 840 West Main Street, Lansdale, PA 19446; (215)362-5070.

Books

Arlie Hochschild, *The Second Shift*, New York: Viking, 1989.

Surgay Songer, M.D. and John Kelly, *The Woman Who Works, The Parent Who Cares: A revolutionary program for raising your child*. Boston: Little, Brown, 1987.

Deborah Swiss and Judith Walker, *Women and the Work Family Dilemma*, New York: Wiley, 1993.

Lise Vogel, *Mothers on the Job*, New Brunswick, NJ: Rutgers University Press, 1993.

Articles

Katharine Esty and Jane Bermont, "Changing Corporate Culture to Support Work and Family Programs," The Bureau of National Affairs, Special Report Series #42, June 1991.

Dana Friedman and Arlene Johnson, "Strategies for Promoting a Work-Family Agenda," The Conference Board, Report #973.

Fran S. Rodgers and Charles Rodgers, "Business and the Facts of Family Life," *Harvard Business Review*, November–December 1989, p. 121, Reprint No. 89610.

Audiovisuals

Another Call from Home, Dartnell, 4660 North Rovenswood Ave., Chicago, IL 60640.

The Power of Diversity: Module VI, Balance of Work/Family Issues, CorVision Media, 1359 Barclay Blvd., Buffalo Grove, IL 60089; (800) 537-3130.

CHAPTER 10

PEOPLE WITH DISABILITIES

THE SUBJECT

> *People have gotten tired of expressions like "differently abled."*
> *Let's face it... I'm a paraplegic, and that's what I am. I'm in a*
> *wheelchair. OK? In America there's an idea that if you come*
> *up with a perfect word you'll never offend anyone. I remember*
> *when my little niece was trying to figure out why her Uncle*
> *John was sitting in a chair all the time. She kept pinching me in*
> *the legs, harder and harder, asking if I could feel it. I'd say no,*
> *no. Then she asked if I would feel a bee sting. When I said no,*
> *she ran to her mother, "Mommy, Uncle John is not afraid of*
> *bees." That's what they should put on the signs in the parking*
> *places: I'm not a disabled person, I'm not physically challenged.*
> *I'm a person who's not afraid of bees.*

So commented John Hockenberry, an ABC correspondent, in a newspaper interview.[1]

An estimated 49 million Americans have a disability. (See
Figure 10.1.) That's close to 20 percent of the population, or one in
every five people. Also, experts estimate there is an 80 percent
chance that an average person will experience some kind of disability
in the course of a lifetime. Most extended families have at least one
member with a disability.

The term *disability* covers a wide range of physical and mental
conditions. We tend to think of problems with walking, seeing, and
hearing, but the word is much broader. (See Figure 10.2.) As the
Federal government defines it, alcoholism, cancer, drug addiction,

---

[1] *Boston Globe Magazine*, June 19, 1994, p. 5.

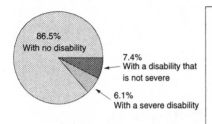

• Alcoholism	• HIV positive
• Cancer	• Mental retardation
• Cerebral palsy	• Muscular distrophy
• Diabetes	• Multiple sclerosis
• Drug addiction	• Orthopedic
• Emotional illness	• Specific learning
• Epilepsy	disability
• Hearing impairments	• Speech impairments
• Heart disease	• Visual impairments

Fig. 10.1 People with Disabilities: 1992
Source: U.S. Bureau of the Census.

Fig. 10.2 Disabilities (Conditions, diseases, and infections that may be classified as physical or mental impairments under the ADA, depending on the severity of the impairment.)

emotional illness, HIV, and learning deficits are all considered disabilities, as are congenital abnormalities, speech problems, and facial disfigurement. The most common disability affecting the workplace is probably back problems.

Using this broad definition, people in the workplace have a large number of disabilities, most of which are entirely invisible to their coworkers. In the future, there will be even more people with disabilities in the workplace. This is due to the rising age of employees; an estimated 46 percent of the population over age sixty-five has a disability, as do many people in their fifties and early sixties. In addition, changing attitudes and new legislation have made it possible for a much larger percentage of people with disabilities to find work. (See Figure 10.3.) This is a trend that will continue.

Some companies, such as the Marriott Corporation, McDonald's, DuPont, Honeywell, and US WEST, proactively seek to hire workers with disabilities. DuPont, which has documented its experience with workers with disabilities over a period of thirty years, reports that persons with disabilities do not differ from other employees in terms of their job performance, their attendance, and their safety records.

"These companies have a hiring bias. They only want the best."
—FROM AN ADVERTISEMENT LISTING CORPORATE CLIENTS OF JUST ONE BREAK, THE LARGEST NONPROFIT EMPLOYMENT AGENCY FOR PEOPLE WITH DISABILITIES

THE LAW

In 1990 the Americans with Disabilities Act (ADA) was passed, legislation that is considered a "Magna Carta" for people with disabilities. Until recently, at least two-thirds of Americans with disabilities were unemployed, and many relied on government assistance in one form or another. One reason for ADA was simply to reduce the costs of providing public support. The legislators hoped to aid business as well. Advocates of persons with disabilities had reported to Congress the increased performance of pioneering companies that had consistently hired people with disabilities in the past.

The intent of ADA is to prohibit discrimination against qualified workers with disabilities who are able to perform essential job functions with or without reasonable accommodation. The law applies to businesses with fifteen or more employees. Unless it creates an excessive or undue hardship on the business, the employer is required to provide any needed accommodation. The law also covers those associated with disabled persons, such as parents of a disabled child or those caring for people infected with AIDS.

"For years, being fair has meant treating everyone the same. Employers are uncomfortable with accommodations because that's treating someone differently."
—CHRISTOPHER G. BELL, FORMER EEOC LAWYER WHO HELPED WRITE ADA RULES

The protection provided by ADA includes all aspects of work: advertising, recruitment, promotion, transfers, rates of pay and other compensation, job assignments, selection for training and special events, sick leave, social and recreational programs, and access to facilities intended for employees.

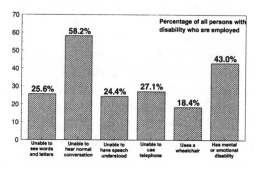

Fig. 10.3 People with Disability Who Work: 1992
Source: U.S. Bureau of the Census.

But there is protection for employers and the business as well. Employers do not have to hire individuals with disabilities who are not qualified for the job, nor do they have to give preference to persons with disabilities over other applicants. Moreover, if a person does not identify himself or herself as having a disability, employers generally do not have to make any accommodation unless the disability is obvious.

The Rehabilitation Act of 1973, which applies to federal contractors, prevents discrimination against individuals with disabilities and has many similarities to the ADA.

The Equal Employment Opportunity Commission, the agency charged with interpreting and enforcing the ADA, has made it clear that persons with disabilities must be granted equal access to health insurance coverage that is offered to other employees. For example, an employer cannot deny health insurance coverage solely on the basis of an employee having a disability.

There are different regulations in place for public accommodations, such as restaurants and stores, which must provide accessibility to the general public under Title III of the ADA.

COMMON ISSUES AND CONCERNS
GETTING A JOB

In our consulting work, we have learned that there is only one major issue for people with disabilities, although there are other issues that are key for managers and supervisors in the workplace. For a person with a visible disability, the major hurdle is landing a job. Repeated experiences of rejection discourage even the most hardy, and, in the past, this was the typical story for persons with a visible disability. Only recently, since the passage of the ADA, have many employers started to seriously consider the applications of such persons.

Some companies are determined to learn whether a job candidate has an invisible disability. All candidates may be subjected to a barrage of questions designed to learn about any preexisting condition or medical problem. (See Figure 10.4.) This is particularly true in recent years because of employer concerns about AIDS. Many companies insist that all candidates have a blood test to determine if they are HIV positive.

Two other conditions, obesity and shortness, are newly being recognized as barriers to employment and promotability. Studies have

Questions that Are Okay to Ask	Questions that Are Not Okay to Ask
Can you perform the functions of this job with or without reasonable accommodation?	Do you have AIDS? Do you have asthma?
Do you have a cold? Have you ever tried Tylenol for fever? How did you break your leg?	How did you become disabled?
Can you meet the attendance requirements of this job?	Have you ever filed for workers' compensation? Have you ever been injured on the job?
How many days did you take leave last year?	How often did you use illegal drugs in the past?
Do you illegally use drugs? Have you used illegal drugs in the last two years?	Have you ever been addicted to drugs?
Do you drink alcohol?	How much alcohol do you drink each week? Have you ever been treated for alcohol problems?
How much do you weigh? How tall are you? Do you regularly eat three meals a day?	Have you ever been treated for mental health problems?
	Have you ever taken AZT? What prescription drugs are you currently taking?

Fig. 10.4 Questions that Are Okay and Not Okay for Employers to Ask People with Disabilities

demonstrated that obesity can have a devastating impact on career advancement. This is particularly true for obese women, whose salaries are on average far lower than those of their more slender counterparts. A recent study found that 33 percent of the overall population is obese. The group with the highest proportion of overweight people was black, non-Hispanic women, 49 percent of whom were obese. Short people have found that their taller coworkers move ahead faster than they do.

"Our experience is that people with disabilities work better than others because they want the job and need it."
—A STATE REHABILITATION AGENCY DIRECTOR

OUR COMMENT

We encourage companies to actively seek employees with disabilities because, as the DuPont study demonstrates, they are good employees. It is easy to be biased against people with disabilities because of worry that they can't do the job, or more often, just because of persistent stereotypes about them. It takes an open mind to give a person with a disability a fair shake, particularly if your company has not made a public commitment to hiring people with disabilities. But we see this as a new frontier that can benefit those in the organization as much as the person with a disability.

Be particularly aware of subtle discrimination against short and obese persons. Stay focused on the job requirements and job performance. Be particularly wary of disqualifying an overweight person on his or her weight alone.

POOR PERFORMANCE

In some work situations, of course, there are people with disabilities who have performance problems. Despite their initial hopes and expectations and those of their employers, their work is unsatisfactory. Managers and supervisors are often uncertain how to handle these problems. They tend to avoid dealing with them as long as possible.

OUR COMMENT

The first step is to start dealing with the situation and to assess what is actually going on. Are the problems a result of the disability, or are they performance problems rooted in some other issue?

The tendency in dealing with people with disabilities is to see them as either saints or sinners. In reality, most of them fall somewhere in between, and like other employees, they will have performance problems from time to time. (See Chart 10.1.) for some guidelines for working with people with disabilities.

> "The worse the communication within the company, the more trouble you will have in dealing with employees with disabilities."
> —TOM O'CONNELL, HR MANAGER AT WANG LABORATORIES

It is vital, then, when there are performance problems, to start talking about the issues, give accurate feedback on the specific issues, and create a plan of action. Possible alternatives include restructuring the job, further training, or transfer to another job, as well as termination. Joint problem solving is almost always a preferred way of dealing with this kind of issue.

In those instances where there are issues involving the disability itself, you might consider bringing in a consultant from an agency that deals with disabilities. He or she can often provide expert counsel and suggest an approach that will be satisfactory to everyone.

MAKING CHANGES / PHYSICAL ACCOMMODATIONS

Many managers' primary worry in hiring a person with disabilities is the expense of accommodation. For example, emotionally they may wish to hire someone who is blind or who uses a wheelchair, but they know that the company is on a tight budget. Rumors of companies being forced into exorbitant capital expenditures for ramps, elevators, and bathrooms often scare off managers.

CHART 10.1

TEN GUIDELINES FOR COMMUNICATING WITH PEOPLE WITH DISABILITIES FROM THE NATIONAL CENTER FOR ACCESS UNLIMITED, CHICAGO, ILLINOIS

1. Treat adults as adults. Address people who have disabilities by their first names only when extending the same familiarity to all others. Never patronize people in wheelchairs by patting them on the head or shoulder.
2. Offer to shake hands when introduced. People with limited hand use or an artificial limb can usually shake hands, and offering the left hand is an acceptable greeting.
3. Always identify yourself and others who may be with you when meeting someone with a visual impairment. When conversing in a group, remember to identify the person to whom you are speaking.
4. If you offer assistance, wait until the offer is accepted. Then listen or ask for instructions.
5. Make eye contact and speak directly to a person who is hearing-impaired, rather than through a companion or sign-language interpreter who may be present.
6. Do not lean against or put your hand on someone's wheelchair. Bear in mind that disabled people in wheelchairs frequently treat their chairs as extensions of their bodies.
7. Listen attentively when talking with people who have difficulty speaking and wait for them to finish. If necessary, ask short questions that require short answers. Never pretend to understand if you are having difficulty doing so. Instead repeat what you have understood and allow the person to respond.
8. Place yourself at eye level when speaking with someone in a wheelchair or on crutches.
9. Tap a hearing-impaired person on the shoulder or wave your hand to get his or her attention. Look directly at the person and speak clearly, slowly, and expressively to find out if the person can read your lips. If so, try to face the light sources and keep hands, cigarettes, and food away from your mouth when speaking.
10. Relax. Don't be embarrassed if you happen to use common expressions such as "See you later," or "Did you hear about this?" that seem to relate to a person's disability.

OUR COMMENT

A study done in 1989 by the federal government presents a quite different picture. Half of all accommodations for people with disabilities cost less than fifty dollars.[2] Tax incentives are often available for companies that do have to spend substantial amounts of money on accommodations.

In many instances, the cost of making changes in physical layout is justified on business grounds. At stake is not merely the functioning of the particular employee, but accessibility of the workplace for others as well. Rehab of the space may well benefit other employees who may become disabled in the future. Furthermore, by not making these changes, a company could be violating the law and putting itself at risk of a lawsuit.

It is also important to realize that if the disability is visible, you are justified in asking during a job interview about the person's ability to perform specific tasks connected with essential functions of the job. Though you can't set phony performance standards, you can certainly ascertain whether the applicant's disability would prevent him or her from being able to do the job. And you can feel free to reject anyone who really can't do the essentials of the job.

FITTING IN

Managers and supervisors tell us that they have concerns about a person with a disability fitting in and becoming a full-fledged member of the team. Often they feel that a person with a disability will drag down production and make everyone feel uncomfortable, including the workgroup, suppliers, customers, and colleagues. They feel that the people in the workgroup would feel obligated to be "nice."

OUR COMMENT

Research has found that most people do avoid being close to those with visible disabilities. They typically choose a seat far away from such a person. Employees often do not make eye contact with such people or greet them nearly as often as they do others. This suggests

---

[2] Data from the President's Committee on Employment of People with Disabilities Job Accommodation Network, which can be contacted at (800) JAN-7234.

that you'll need to prepare your people when you do hire a person with a disability. Research has also found that tension is dramatically diminished if people are able to talk about the disability. This is, of course, a two-way street, but in our experience the person with the disability is usually quite comfortable with his or her situation and welcomes acknowledgment of what is an obvious fact. Once it is mentioned, people can get on with the job.

"The only real disability is ignorance."
—ITT HARTFORD AD

WORKING EXAMPLES
THE EMPLOYEE WITH AIDS

Shep Woods has AIDS. Shep, who is employed by a small company, operates a bindery machine that folds printed material. He works on the shop floor along with a dozen other machine operators. Two years ago, when Shep discovered he was HIV positive, he told his coworkers. More recently, he has been diagnosed as having AIDS and has missed several weeks of work.

Some of his fellow workers are paranoid about catching the disease from Shep. Two employees have complained to Marc, their supervisor, that they should not have to work near someone who has AIDS. They refuse to touch Shep's machine and say they consider him a serious danger to themselves and their families.

OUR COMMENT

Marc knows that AIDS is a disability protected by law. But he has a serious morale problem on his hands along with the question of how much longer Shep can really do his job. We suggest that Marc bring in resource people from a local organization to provide a training session on AIDS. Some companies' EAPs provide such programs. The training session can offer information on how AIDS can be transmitted. But the employees need more than the facts about AIDS. They need a chance to discuss their own feelings and have their concerns taken seriously. Only then will they be able to move beyond them. They also need to be reminded of Shep's right to his job. Often it is useful to go over the company's policy on AIDS with everyone. If no policy exists, Marc needs to urge Human Resources or senior management to develop one right away.

Marc needs to sit down with Shep on a regular basis to discuss his plans and assess together his work schedule. We suggest that they meet on a weekly basis. Shep may try to keep working way past the time he can actually do the job. Often, however, the problem solves itself without intervention by the company.

CHRONIC COMPLAINER

Sally Ianello, who works as a secretary for a large law firm, has just returned to the workplace after a long absence bringing up children. For the past ten years she has used a wheelchair. Though highly skilled with the computer, Sally is full of complaints. Her chair does not allow her sufficient leg room, she says, despite several efforts by the maintenance department to adjust it to an appropriate height. The door to the restroom is too hard for her to push open, and she finds the elevator up from the company's parking garage difficult to manage. To her confidants in the office, Sally claims that the bosses have no concern for her. "They don't like having someone like me to deal with," she charges, "and are just waiting for the chance to sack me."

OUR COMMENT

Solving this problem requires an accurate assessment. Does Sally have a bad attitude, or are her complaints sensible? We think the first step is to review Sally's complaints one by one and see what can be done to make her more comfortable. Part of the issue may be Sally's adjustment to the workplace. If the complaints continue, think about putting her in touch with another employee with a disability, either in the office or from another company. If no good candidate for this informal counseling role is in sight, refer her to your EAP or to an outside agency experienced in working with people with disabilities.

THE NEWLY DISCOVERED DISABILITY

Richard Gutmann has worked more than twenty years for a retail hardware store chain. He travels to various outlets in a six-state area to ensure that inventory is appropriate and to handle problems for subsidiaries. Recently, however, it was discovered that Richard has an inoperable back problem, and he has been unable to work on eighteen days in the last three months. His supervisor, Mario, feels that Richard can no longer be relied upon to do his job and wants to let him go.

Richard has let it be known that if the company follows through on its threat, he will sue. He has told Mario that he has already hired a lawyer and will claim that he is covered by the ADA.

OUR COMMENT

In 1993, more than 15,000 people filed complaints with the federal Equal Employment Opportunity Commission, charging discrimination under ADA. One of them, an employee with an inoperable brain tumor, sued the employer that was threatening to fire him and was awarded over $500,000. The outcome of this lawsuit underscores the need for managers to tread cautiously. Many managers have felt at a loss in dealing with cases like this one. At stake are loyalty and friendship, as well as bottom-line issues. Usually there are no easy answers. The best solutions are usually developed via negotiations and creative problem solving among the manager, Human Resources, and the employee in question. This might mean changing the job, creating more flexible working conditions, or finding another position for him.

QUESTIONS AND ANSWERS

Q: Last year, Rico, who is in my workgroup at a factory that makes Jeeps, was injured by a forklift. I believe he was on drugs. After being out on disability, he's back at work again after five months. People are upset because they had to do extra work while he was out and because they think he is often careless about safety.

A: Have a discussion with Rico and let him know what you expect from him from now on. Also talk to others in the group. If they are, indeed, angry at Rico, you may need to take additional steps to clear the air and to discuss safety issues. Inform your workgroup about the company's policy on disabilities so that they understand the ground rules.

Q: Recently I hired a woman with epilepsy. She is going to start work next week. Should I tell employees about her condition?

A: It all depends. Sit down with the employee and ask what you need to know about her disability and what others need to know. You may wish to ask your state rehabilitation agency for expert advice. It may be that your other employees will need training in the specifics of epilepsy, or it may be that there is no need for them to even know about her condition. It should be a joint decision.

Q: I just interviewed a young man with a disability. I know my work site can accommodate his disability, but I still feel anxious about hiring him. I'd be his direct supervisor, and I'm afraid that if the need arose, I'd feel awkward criticizing his performance.

A: This is a very common concern. Mikki Lam, executive director of Just One Break, in New York City, an agency that places individuals with disabilities, urges managers and supervisors to conduct business as usual. "The disabled don't come with halos," she notes. "If they aren't doing a good job, they need to know it—and, if necessary, be fired like any other worker if they don't shape up."

Q: I'm the owner of a small new business and am operating on a shoestring budget. I'd like to hire disabled workers, but I'm concerned about the cost of adapting my setup for their needs. Isn't it going to be expensive to accommodate disabled workers?

A: The facts here are really encouraging. Statistics show that most workplace accommodations are not costly; 15 percent actually cost employers nothing. Although employers tend to think initially about major architectural changes, which can be costly, there are many creative, inexpensive things that can be done to enable people with physical disabilities to work effectively. One employer we know called in a counselor from a local agency that deals extensively with work issues for people with disabilities because a researcher who required a wheelchair was working too slowly. The counselor's simple suggestion—to place the researcher's files on a table the same height as her desk—enabled her to move around in her wheelchair much less frequently and doubled her output! Other inexpensive adjustments, from lowering shelves to using carousel files, can make formerly difficult tasks routine for some workers.

Q: As the director of human resources for a company that is eager to hire the best possible talent, I am interested in including people with disabilities in our applicant pools as often as possible. I'm not much of a technical wizard, but it seems to me that with so many wonderful new technologies being developed, there ought to be potential solutions to some of the impediments that currently prevent workers with some types of disabilities from joining our ranks. Am I heading in the right direction?

A: Absolutely. A variety of applications of new technologies are opening up opportunities for people with disabilities. These range from remote-control devices that allow employees in wheelchairs to open doors to special telephone systems for the hearing impaired. Computers are also being adapted for people with sight and motor disabilities. Identifying these technical solutions may require outside assistance; organizations such as the International Center for the Disabled in New York City can provide such a resource.

Q: One of the sales associates in the store I manage has been diagnosed as having cancer. She tells me she will be undergoing chemotherapy. I feel sorry for her, but I am worried. I need consistent coverage of the floor. What should I do?

A: Many of the work schedules that have been developed relatively recently to assist employees in balancing work and family responsibilities—flex time, job sharing, part-time options—can be effectively utilized to enable employees with a variety of life-threatening illnesses (including AIDS) to continue to work while undergoing medical treatments. One Boston restaurant owner we heard about adjusted the schedules of two chefs because one of them was undergoing chemotherapy, and she did not want to lose her talented employee. This sort of adaptation makes a lot of sense. A valued, loyal worker is a tremendous resource, and not one lightly dismissed. It usually is a lot more efficient, cost-effective, and humane to juggle schedules a bit to permit employees the latitude they need so that they can continue to work during these difficult periods.

Q: My new boss uses a wheelchair. Should I open doors for him and things like that?

A: One of the hidden challenges of integrating workers with disabilities into the workplace is that employees face daily dilemmas regarding logistics and etiquette. Disabled workers and their colleagues and supervisors need to learn how to communicate with each other about these issues, and, once again, outside experts may need to be brought in to educate everyone. As a rule of thumb, however, don't assume that you know what a disabled worker would appreciate in the way of assistance. Ask the person.

Q: George, sixty, has had a poor attendance record ever since he began working in my shop. Now he's claiming that he has a "heart condition" and is "disabled." Even when he does come to work, he refuses to do certain chores, claiming disability. How much of this do I have to take?

A: George may or may not be qualified for disabled status; he needs to go through a formal process to determine this. Urge him to go to Human Resources to learn about the specific in your organization. Disabled status is not just a self-created designation.

Q: My secretary broke her leg skiing. Can she use the handicapped spaces in the parking lot until her leg heals?

A: Assuming that you are talking about a parking lot on private property, you should check with whoever sets the policy for the facility. This is probably either your company or its landlord. Inquire about "temporary" handicapped arrangements, and whether your secretary would need a special sticker, pass, or dashboard card announcing her status.

ACTION STEPS THAT WORK

1. Since the greatest single problem for people with disabilities is the stigma of being different, create an atmosphere in which they can feel accepted. In this way, you will get better job performance from them.

2. Talk to Human Resources about whether your company has a commitment to hiring people with disabilities. If you are open to the idea, tell them. Have a training session on ADA for yourself and coworkers. It's important to understand the law of the workplace.
3. Have regular meetings with any employees who have disabilities, especially in their first months on the job.
4. Consult an expert in this field; it's amazing what valuable information one can learn from people with extensive experience in working with those who have disabilities.
5. Show a film about AIDS in the workplace.

CREATING COMPETITIVE ADVANTAGE

Do's	Don'ts
• Do refer to "people with disabilities," rather than "disabled persons" or "the disabled."	• Don't use terms like "cripples" or "handicapped people."
• Do ask a person with a disability how he or she wishes to describe it.	• Don't avoid normal contact with people with disabilities.
• Do call on outside agencies for advice and education.	• Don't assume that a person with a disability wants special coddling.
• Do deal with any performance problems as soon as possible.	• Don't rule out hiring a person with a disability without careful consideration of his or her situation.

RESOURCES

ORGANIZATIONS

The President's Committee on Employment of People with Disabilities; 1331 F St. N.W., Washington, DC 20004; (202) 543-6353. Offers valuable free materials on disabilities and employment issues.

Governor's Commission on Employment of People with Disabilities. Every state has an agency with this or a similar name that provides information, referral, and other services to employers as well as individuals.

Rehabilitation Commissions in every state. (There are more than 80 such agencies. Some have separate offices for the blind, etc.)

Job Accommodation Network; (800) 872-2253. Gives free advice about physical changes in the workplace.

BOOKS

Timothy L. Jones, *The Americans with Disabilities Act: A Review of Best Practices*, New York: American Management Association, 1993.

Thomas D. Schneid, *The Americans with Disabilities Act: A Practical Guide for Managers*, New York: Van Nostrand Reinhold, 1992.

Tilting at Windmills, a notebook with 15 different modules that include games and exercises, Chatsworth, CA: Milt Wright Associates; (818) 349-0858.

ARTICLES

Laura M. Livan, "The Disabilities Law: Avoid the Pitfalls," *Nation's Business*, January 1994, vol. 82, no. 1, p. 25.

Catharine Yang, "Business Has to Find a New Meaning for Fairness," *Business Week*, April 12, 1993, p. 72.

AUDIOVISUAL MATERIALS

Persons with Disabilities: Making the Workplace Inclusive, The National Conference of Christians and Jews Northeastern Region, 15 Broad St., Suite 505, Boston, MA 02109. This forty-minute video comes with a facilitator's guide.

Part of the Team, The National Easter Seal Society, Communications Department, 70 East Lake Street, Chicago, IL 60601. A video produced by the IBM Corporation in cooperation with the National Easter Seal Society and the President's Committee on Employment of People with Disabilities.

The Power of Diversity: Module II; Disabilities: Hiring and Promotion. CorVision Media, 1359 Barclay Blvd., Buffalo Grove, IL 60089; (800) 537-3130.

CHAPTER 11

WHITE MEN

THE SUBJECT

Sometimes I feel bashed. When I call someone "honey", for instance, I get angry looks. Then when I deliberately try to be thoughtful, like the day I bought roses for my secretary, I got a "raises not roses speech" in response from a woman manager I work with. I feel like I can't do anything right!
—White male engineer in Spokane

I can now acknowledge the privileges and advantages I have had as a white man. I am aware that I may be the recipient of unintended preferential treatment by my peers and managers.
—White male foreman in Maine

THESE two quotes suggest the range in the experience of what it means to be a white man in the workplace today. Despite the influx of diverse workers since the 1970s, white men are still the largest single group in the U.S. labor force. (See Figure 11.1.) They make up 47 percent of the total workforce, and number more than 57 million. By the year 2005, white men will still constitute 44 percent of those employed, despite all the hoopla about the changing workforce and growing diversity in the country.

"I have yet to see the need for affirmative action for white males at my company."
—TOM O'CONNELL, HUMAN RESOURCES DIRECTOR, WANG LABORATORIES

What makes white men different from other groups is one fact. They have traditionally held almost all of the power in the United States, shaping our key institutions—educational, financial, scientific, governmental, industrial, cultural, and religious. White males

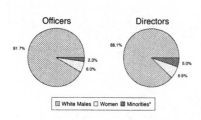

Fig. 11.1 White Males Still Running Corporate
America: 1993
Source: U.S. Bureau of Labor Statistics.

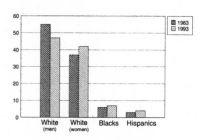

Fig. 11.2 White Men as a Percentage of
Managerial and Professional Workers
Source: U.S. Bureau of Labor Statistics.

remain the key policy makers and chief executives across the country. (See Figure 11.2.) More than 99 percent of the CEOs of the Fortune 500 companies are white men.

White men hold almost 50 percent of the managerial and professional jobs today. But they have a somewhat smaller percentage of these jobs than they did in 1983, and, for many men, it seems like white men are moving backwards. (See Figure 11.3.)

In the past, the white man was considered so much the norm that everyone else in the workforce was labeled "nontraditional." Of course, there is much diversity among white men themselves: differences in age, religion, ethnicity, sexual preference, class, level in the organization, educational achievement, and family circumstances. Perhaps because of their history as the overwhelming majority in the workplace and their power, few white men label themselves as white males when thinking about their personal identity. Only recently have they even begun to consider white men as a group.

Today, however, a significant number of white males in the workforce report feeling some pain. They complain that they were born at the wrong time as companies downsize and cut out levels of middle management. Some hearken back nostalgically to an earlier era when it was easy to get a well-paying job and hold it for life. One man describes the plight of white men as akin to being on a shrinking ice floe. Jobs are disappearing, and they must hold on for dear life.

At the same time, some women and people of color hold white men responsible for a system that has held them back. Some white men feel stereotyped, blamed for something created by their fathers and grandfathers. Not only do they see their opportunities as increasingly limited, but also, for the first time, white men feel the sting of being lumped in a group. Recent attention to the issue of sexual harassment has added to the feelings of some white men that they are under siege. To avoid getting in trouble, they must be ever vigilant. Kidding around, as in the old days, has become too risky.

In spite of everything above, many white men are going along happily, more or less aware that they are living through a social revolution. They try to be fair toward others who seek a place at the table of power. But they themselves want to be treated fairly and wish to be recognized for their abilities. They feel that no one has a right to a job or a promotion on the basis of color or gender. They tell us that they want everyone to be treated fairly, but that they are opposed to affirmative action, quotas, and sacrificing quality.

THE LAW

White males, per se, are not a protected class. However, the same basic laws that protect other employees also protect them. Title VII of the Civil Rights Act of 1964 prohibits employment discrimination against anyone based on race, color, religion, sex, or national origin. Thus, a white male who is denied employment because of his race, religion, or gender could bring suit under federal law and under many state laws. Title VII also protects white men in that it prohibits retaliation against people who file charges of discrimination or oppose an unlawful employment practice.

Fig. 11.3 White Men as a Percentage of the Civilian Labor Force: 1970, 1980 & 1990
Source: U.S. Bureau of Labor Statistics.

The Equal Pay Act prohibits employers from discriminating between men and women on the basis of sex in the payment of wages when they perform substantially equal work under similar working conditions in the same establishment. The law also prohibits employers from reducing the wages of either sex to comply with the law. Though passed to protect women, this law obviously covers men as well.

Finally, every state has laws that protect the rights of employees, including white males. You need to be sure you are aware of those that affect you and your workgroup.

COMMON ISSUES AND CONCERNS

One of the surprises we find in running focus groups in organizations across the country is the degree to which many white men in today's workplace are hurting. In the following section, we discuss three major issues concerning them.

THE RULES OF THE GAME ARE CHANGING

Many white males feel at sea at work, no longer sure they understand what the company values in its employees. They see their own opportunities for advancement as shrinking; at the same time, they observe their organizations putting tremendous effort into hiring and promoting a more diverse group of employees. Sometimes they feel that their hard work over many years has not been recognized by their organization. Many white men do not see or understand any business imperative for diversity and believe affirmative action to be totally unfair. They just aren't sure what the rules are any more.

> "Toto, I've a feeling we're not in Kansas anymore."
> —*WIZARD OF OZ* SCREENPLAY.

OUR COMMENT

Managers and supervisors need to take these kinds of concerns on the part of white men seriously. There is actually quite a lot you can do to help. First, explain to your entire workgroup exactly what the company policies are regarding EEO and affirmative action. Make the rules of the game as public as possible. Second, when you talk about diversity, use language that includes white men and use terms that do not create divisions between "us" and "them." Take the time to explain the business case for diversity in your organization. If you can't make a strong case, ask Human Resources or your boss to assist. You can consider forming support groups for white men. It may still sound odd to have such groups for white males, but some companies (AT&T and Motorola, for example) have found value in them.

STALLED CAREERS

New workplace priorities have had the effect of putting the careers of some white males on hold. Many of them feel that they have been passed over for promotion in favor of women and minority males. Many white men, in fact, believe that they have limited opportunity to advance and that they face a bleak future. When they believe themselves to be far more qualified than those who do get promoted, the hurt is deep. Some white men blame EEO and affirmative action for their limited opportunities. They talk about injustice, and they feel varying degrees of anger. They note that the earnings of white men have actually been shrinking since 1970.

OUR COMMENT

What is often not recognized is that much of the limited opportunity is a result of downsizing. It is the economic situation, not diversity, that has changed things. Hundreds of thousands of jobs have been eliminated at companies like IBM, Aetna, United Airlines, Apple Computer, and Digital.

To this day, white men retain most senior management positions. At one midwestern manufacturing company, for example, 135 of the top 145 executives are white men. In spite of these numbers, we were told over and over how well women were doing. There were even a number of comments such as, "Women are taking over this company." It seemed that when even a small handful of women achieved senior management status, it was perceived as a threat by some white men.

Management does owe employees as much information about their prospects as possible. Each company should have its policies on diversity and affirmative action available to all. In particular, assurance that there are no quotas or designated affirmative action positions is needed. Most white men want to believe that if they keep their skills well honed, stay open to new ways of doing business, and accept the rights of people different from themselves to also advance, the company will still value them.

Career development programs are one positive avenue for dealing with limited opportunity. Is information on what is needed to move ahead made available to employees in your organization? The major complaint of women and people of color is still that too many hiring decisions depend on who you know. This can hurt many white men, too. Some organizations have found that when they expand their job posting systems and better utilized existing data banks, talented and appropriate candidates—both men and women, white and people of color—emerge for consideration.

CAN'T YOU TAKE A JOKE?
Some white men tell us that the workplace just isn't as much fun as it used to be. They have to be so careful about sexual harassment that they feel they're walking on eggshells. They can't make jokes or compliment women, and they certainly can't fondle a woman ever. "The pendulum has swung too far," one frustrated manager told us. "I'm on guard all the time. I'd never dare ask a young woman to lunch anymore; people would talk."

Many white men are discovering that something they've always thought of as friendly or funny is offensive to somebody else. Some employees resent being told to take down their pin-up calendars; others are surprised when they are asked to stop sending dirty jokes around via E-mail. A few white men reminisce about earlier days when sales conferences were all-male events and it was a lot of fun "being with the boys." Today stag events in the workplace are rare. Even holiday parties are more apt to be alcohol-free events in the cafeteria than cocktails and dinner in a fancy restaurant.

> "It's a new kind of McCarthyism. White men are scared that if they complain they'll be tagged as racist and sexist. To complain is to confirm the stereotype."
> —FREDERICK LYNCH, *BOSTON GLOBE,* NOVEMBER 22, 1992

OUR COMMENT
While some men are nostalgic for the way things were, the reality is that the world has changed. Many men like the changes; they never did feel comfortable with dirty jokes and graphic language about women. Clearly, a major challenge for the 1990s is to develop a kind of humor and fun in the workplace that does not come at anyone else's expense. At Ben and Jerry's, for example, they have a "joy gang,"

whose task it is to think up events and activities that will be fun for employees.

Still, the new work environment is experienced as not like "the good old days" by many. We, by the way, do not believe that the pendulum has swung too far. In our consultation with organizations, we still hear reports that demonstrate disrespectful treatment of women and others. For example, toward the end of one company's 1993 holiday party, the white male, CEO mooned the assembled throng. At another company's golf outing, there were strippers stationed at several places on the course to provide entertainment to the passing golfers.

WORKING EXAMPLES
STYMIED EXECUTIVE

Fred Kosucowski once seemed to be on the fast track. Ten years ago, he was widely regarded by his insurance company as a star, with the potential for rising high and fast. Something seems to have happened to his bright career prospects, however. Now, at age fifty-one, Fred seems burned out. He puts in his hours but seems more interested in talking than in doing the job, according to his coworkers.

Fred traces the problem back to an incident that happened eighteen months ago. At that time he was being considered for promotion to vice president. Though he was one of two finalists for this promotion, he was ultimately passed over. The job went to a relative newcomer, a woman.

Everybody who deals with him has noticed his bitterness: peers, subordinates, and long-standing customers. Fred just cannot reconcile himself to seeing an "pushy young woman" in the position that he feels should have been his. Fred's manager wonders what he can do to turn Fred around and get him back on track. The company still needs his experience; it would be costly to let him go.

OUR COMMENT

Thinking of this as a career development problem, not a diversity issue, is what's critical here. Fred's manager needs to work with him to reframe his predicament in that light. Fred may need a new challenge. His manager might explore a number of alternatives with him: a lateral move, changing jobs within his current division, restructuring his job, transferring to another division, or getting an assignment to a new project. People can look incompetent when they feel stuck. We think a turnaround may be possible if Fred is given a new opportunity and clear guidelines for acceptable performance.

REAL MEN DON'T DO THAT

Jason Rosenbaum, a young manager in a utilities company, has a wife who has a job in a PR firm. They divide responsibilities for the kids, and Jason's task is to pick them up at day care. This means Jason has to leave work every day at exactly 5:15 to arrive in time to get them. It is also known that Jason does most of the cooking at home. Jason's boss has told him that he is concerned about Jason's lack of commitment to his career. This concern seems focused on day-care pickup. Jason has also urged the president of the company to promote a talented young woman to head the Customer Service Division, even though most of the other managers have told the president she is too young for the job.

OUR COMMENT

It is important to realize that there are many Jasons in the workplace: white men who are trying to manage their jobs and share child-rearing responsibilities. They may also be working for a more inclusive workplace. These men can face difficulties, depending on the culture of their particular workplace. Sometimes this takes the form of some gentle ribbing, but they can face discrimination if their bosses hold rigid views about gender roles. In Jason's case, we talked to his boss several times over a one-year period. It was nip and tuck whether Jason would get a long-awaited promotion because of the perception of his lack of commitment. It is safe to say that without our intervention, he would have been passed over.

THE "HEROIC MANAGER"

Tom McNair seems to have everything going for him. He usually spends sixty or seventy hours at the office each week, plus added time doing paperwork at home. At the same time, however, Tom is described as cold by his direct reports, most of whom are women. For example, he never says "good morning" to anyone; he just hurries into his office and turns on his computer. He rarely talks to his staff directly; instead, he usually sends them messages by E-mail. His staff's efforts to assume more responsibility and decrease Tom's workload have come to nothing.

Recently Tom has seemed stressed, and his boss is concerned about his well-being. But he has rebuffed efforts by fellow managers to talk about ways of reducing the pressures.

OUR COMMENT

Tom has risen to his current level in the organization by dint of hard work and long hours. Allan Cohen and David Bradford, in their book *Managers for Excellence,* call this kind of person a "heroic manager." There are still plenty of Toms in the workplace, men who have not yet got the message about developing their staff as well as doing the job. Today's managers need to focus on the quality of their relationships with their people.

Dale Nelson, who worked for many years as an engineer at DuPont and later as a trainer in the company's diversity programs, believes that the best way to work with people like Tom is to provide special training for them. His training program for white men begins with an examination of individual differences in work styles, using an instrument called the Myers Briggs Type Indicator (MBTI). Later he tackles issues such as gender, race, and age. Nelson works with white men by providing them with new information.

We have found that white men have more difficulty than other groups in imagining what the work experience is like for people different from themselves. Most white men are not socialized to be aware of their own feelings or to be tuned into the feelings of others. This, combined with often being in positions of power, leaves them unaware of the dynamics in the workgroup. We have found the model of "one-up, one-down" to be very enlightening to white men and everybody else in explaining the difference in experience between white men and others. Many of the issues that can look like issues of gender are really issues of difference in power.

"Like most white men, I live my life sensing little need to know my feelings or how my behavior impacts women or people of color. I often feel threatened and confused about the negative impact of behavior because I never consciously intend to hurt or oppress anyone."
—ROB NEAL, ORGANIZATIONAL DEVELOPMENT PRACTITIONER

Questions and Answers

Q: I am a middle manager in an aerospace company. Our budget has recently been cut, and at the same time the agency has brought in diversity training in a big way. We now have a director of diversity, and a ton of money is being spent on this stuff. Last week one of my reports, whose name is Joe, attended a two-day mandatory diversity awareness training program. Joe thought it was pretty Mickey Mouse. What really galled him, though, was that it was basically an exercise in white male bashing. What can I do?

A: We suggest that you urge Joe to inform the director of diversity programs about his reaction to the program. There may or may not have been "bashing," but it needs to be checked out. While Joe may be simply demonstrating resistance to change, it is also possible that the quality of the workshop was poor. It is important that organizations be vigilant about the excellence of training and other initiatives related to diversity. While everyone appreciates good intentions, diversity initiatives should not become sacred cows that cannot be criticized or evaluated.

Q: Is the anger of white males justified? How are they faring? What does research show about this?

A: Many white men feel that they are being unjustly stereotyped as the bad guys. They feel that their views, especially on diversity, are being discounted and people presume they don't have as much depth of experience as others. However, in some ways men are moving backwards. Federal government data, analyzed by researchers at Harvard University and MIT, show that the incomes of college-educated males aged forty-five to fifty-four, the overwhelming majority of them white, fell by 17 percent (adjusted for inflation) between 1986 and 1992. (See Figure 11.4.) This marks a turning point, the first time since World War II that people who graduated from college have experienced a serious drop in wages. White men, however, continue to make considerably more than women, dollar for dollar. In fact, for every dollar a man makes, a woman earns only 77 cents.

"'White male' is what I call the newest swear word in America."
—HARRIS SUSSMAN, DIVERSITY CONSULTANT

Q: In terms of company morale and productivity, isn't the risk of backlash from efforts to reform white males greater than the benefits to be gained? In my company I think more harm than good is coming out of the push for women and minorities.

A: The question needs reframing. Diversity does not aim at "reforming white males." Supporting diversity means creating a level playing field for everyone, including white men. As always, the business goal is competitive advantage. The real argument for diversity is getting an edge in an era of heightened competition. And what is more, that very diversity is already here: your job is to manage it productively. The fact that giving everyone a fair shake is also the right thing to do can't be ignored either. A professor of sociology sees it this way: "We like to exaggerate the challenge we face, to talk about reverse discrimination, because it plays down our power. People may bash us, but it's like light rain. It doesn't really affect us.... We still run the country."

Q: Women and people of color keep telling me that, as a white male, I'm privileged. It's hard for me to see exactly what they mean. How can I get more understanding of this issue?

A: All of us have a lot to learn about how others see us. There are a number of resources at the end of this chapter that may be helpful to you. We'd particularly urge you to check out Peggy MacIntosh's piece "White Privilege"—it's a great eye-opener!

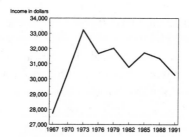

Fig. 11.4 Diminishing Earnings of White Males Who Work Full Time, Year-Round: 1967-1991
Source: U.S. Bureau of the Census.

Q: I think of myself as quite liberal; I believe I treat women and minorities without prejudice. Why should my career be limited because of the mistakes of others in the past?

A: Most career limitation today comes from downsizing, not affirmative action; however, we are in a transitional stage of opening up opportunities for groups that previously have been discriminated against. A part of this activity involves efforts to hire more women and minorities. But most companies seek to be fair, and to hire the best person for the job.

Q: I set up a leadership lecture series for my company, in which two of the eighteen speakers were women. My boss is upset; she says I should have gotten more of a gender balance. What do you think?

A: Sorry, but we agree. Consider extending the series, or double up on speakers, or make panel discussions instead, but diversify!

Q: Four men in my company have just filed a sexual harassment complaint against one of the plant managers, who is a woman. How can this be possible?

A: Harassment is not limited to males harassing females. Since power is so often an element in these cases, and men are frequently in more powerful positions, the problem often involves men harassing women, but this is not always the case. And, of course, some harassment cases involve complaints by men about another man or women complaining about another woman.

Q: As a white male, I feel as if I'm walking on a tightrope. I don't know if I should open doors for my female coworkers or if I should offer to carry heavy equipment? Can I say they look great? Help!

A: A lot of people are feeling confused about appropriate behavior at work these days. One general rule we can give you in this rapidly changing venue is: If in doubt, ask the individual person whether something is okay or offensive. You can also ask your human resources department for a copy of the company policy, and suggest that more training on how to behave is needed for everyone. We have found that there are many grey areas, and almost everyone needs some clarification of what's out of line today.

Q: I'm a white male married to a Hispanic female. I think I'm probably more sensitive to issues of racism than most, yet people treat me like an ignorant clod. I resent this!

A: And with good reason! Just because an individual is a white male doesn't mean that he is any less sensitive than anyone else. Each individual is entitled to be assumed to be prejudice-free until he or she proves otherwise.

ACTION STEPS THAT WORK

1. Inform yourself and others, including white men, about your organization's specific EEO and affirmative action policies. Discuss them with your workgroup so that they are clear about what is policy and what is hearsay.

2. Minimize scapegoating of diversity on the part of white men by pointing out that most of the lack of opportunity in the workplace has resulted not from increased diversity, but from the impact of economic pressures and downsizing.

3. Explain to your workgroup the business case for diversity in your company.

4. Provide training in sexual harassment that gives people a good grounding in the law, in what is acceptable behavior, and in the complaint process.

5. Have a career conversation with each individual in your workgroup to find out who is seeking more challenge and responsibilities.

CREATING COMPETITIVE ADVANTAGE

Do's	Don'ts
• Do express you own commitment to diversity. As a manager, you are a role model.	• Don't assume that all white males share the same views on diversity.
• Do talk about flexibility with your staff and explore how to manage more flexibility in your setting.	• Don't be surprised when you meet resistance to diversity from white males. Surface the resistance and listen carefully.
• Do read this book and discuss it with your coworkers.	• Don't let disrespectful comments go without a response.
• Do focus on career development programs as a good way to provide opportunity for all, including white men.	• Don't accept a candidate list that is limited to white men. Go back and look further.

RESOURCES

ORGANIZATIONS

The Conference Board, 845 Third Ave., New York, NY 10022; (212) 339-0390.

NTL Institute, 1240 N. Pitt St., Suite 100, Alexandria, NJ 22314; (703) 548-8840. Offers training in interpersonal relations and diversity, with special groups for white men.

BOOKS

Anthony Astrachan, *How Men Feel: Their Response to Women's Demands for Equality and Power*, New York: Anchor Press, Doubleday, 1986.

Carol Pierce and Bill Page, *A Male/Female Continuum: Paths to Colleagueship*, 21 Shore Drive, Laconia, NH 03246: New Dynamics Publications, 1990.

Judith Katz, *White Awareness*, Norman: University of Oklahoma, 1978.

Susan L. Webb, *Step Forward: Sexual Harassment in the Workplace. What you need to know.* New York: A Mastermedia Book, 1991.

Robert Stuart Weiss, *Staying the Course: The Emotional and Social Lives of Men Who Do Well at Work*, New York: Free Press, 1990.

ARTICLES

Michelle Galan and Anne Therese Palmer, "White, Male, and Worried," *Business Week*, January 31, 1994, pp. 50–55.

Joseph Potts, "Can White Men Help?" *The Diversity Factor*, Spring 1993, pp. 16–20.

Charlene Marmer Solomon, "Are White Males Being Left Out?" *Personnel Journal*, Vol. 70, November 1991, pp. 88–94.

Duncan Spelman, "White Men and Managing Diversity," *The Diversity Factor*, Spring 1993, pp. 8–15.

AUDIOVISUAL

The Fairer Sex, CorVision Media, 1359 Barclay Blvd., Buffalo Grove, IL 60089; (800) 537-3130.

The Tale of O, On Being Different in an Organization, Goodmeasure, Inc., Cambridge, MA; (617) 621-3838.

The Power of Diversity, Module I,; Reverse Discrimination and Ageism, CorVision Media, 1359 Barclay Blvd., Buffalo Grove, IL 60089; (800) 537-3130.

CHAPTER 12

THE BIGGER PICTURE: CHANGING CORPORATE CULTURE AND ORGANIZATIONAL SYSTEMS TO SUPPORT DIVERSITY

EVERYTHING in this book so far is intended to be useful to managers and supervisors who are doers, working on the front line and dealing with the dilemmas of diversity day to day. We have not assumed that our readers were in a position to change policies or to shape the strategic direction of the organization. The action steps suggested in Chapters 2 through 11 were designed to be implemented by a manager or supervisor, usually without getting permission from a boss, Human Resources, or the CEO.

We couldn't resist, however, adding a chapter that looks at the *big picture* of diversity in the workplace. It is useful for managers and supervisors to increase their understanding of the systemic perspective. It is important to learn how corporate culture and organizational systems, both formal and informal, can support diversity, or, conversely, how these systems can perpetuate a work environment in which people who are different remain clustered at the bottom of the organizational ranks. We think the bigger picture will increase your ability to leverage your actions and become an agent of change.

CORPORATE CULTURE: A DEFINITION

Corporate culture can be defined as "a system of informal rules that spells out how people are to behave most of the time." Others describe corporate culture with such phrases as, "the way we do things around here," "people's customary behavior," "taken-for-granted ways of seeing the world," and "shared assumptions."[1]

---

[1] Terence E. Deal and Alan A. Kennedy, *Corporate Culture: The Rites and Rituals of Corporate Life*, Reading, MA: Addison-Wesley, 1982; p. 15.

You can learn about an organization's culture by observing these unwritten rules in action: how people interact with one another, how they dress, what the workplace humor is, what happens at lunchtime, etc. The stories people tell about the organization, that is, its myths and legends, are one of the best ways to learn about the culture. These stories are one way in which the culture is passed on to new generations of employees, and they reveal clearly what the organization truly values.

ORGANIZATIONAL SYSTEMS: FORMAL AND INFORMAL

There are formal and informal systems in every organization. Management, which consists of senior executives, perhaps a board of directors, middle managers, and supervisors, makes policy, sets the strategic direction, and is the decision-making group. This is a formal leadership system.

The informal system is the way policies and decisions are actually implemented. Often there is a big gap between how things should be done, according to policy, and the actual day-to-day practices. For example, one organization has a very liberal parental leave policy that allows fathers as well as mothers to take paid leave of up to six months. In practice, however, no man has ever taken advantage of this option. As it was explained to us, it would be the "kiss of death" for his career advancement.

There are numerous other policies and practices that can work to create either an organization that appreciates differences or one that perpetuates the status quo.

ORGANIZATIONAL SYSTEMS THAT CAN SUPPORT DIVERSITY	
Orientation programs	Work assignment
Training programs	processes
Decision making	Career development
Performance appraisal	systems
system	Rewards and recognition
Feedback and coaching	Recruitment and hiring
	Planning process

SYSTEMIC AND INDIVIDUAL CHANGE: WHAT IS THE DIFFERENCE?

Organizations fall somewhere along a continuum that ranges from exclusive, essentially monocultural clubs to inclusive organizations that truly value diversity. (See Figure 12.1.)

Today exclusive clubs are few and far between, although there still are organizations that give only lip service to inclusion, or that have only a few token people who are different by gender and race. Many boards of directors and senior management groups are also essentially, nondiverse although the organization as a whole may have many diverse workers in the middle and lower echelons.

The good news is that so many companies are making efforts to become multicultural. Although, in many cases, these efforts were originally spurred by the EEO and affirmative action laws, the companies have now become convinced that diversity will help their businesses.

Some of these efforts to diversify focus on changing individual attitudes and mindsets, whereas others focus on the organizational systems. Some senior managers already have goodwill in terms of diversity, i.e., they have the intention of being fair and supporting diverse employees. What's holding things back, they conclude, is the organizational culture and its systems which still inadvertently tend to perpetuate a bias favoring the "old boys."

For example, much hiring still depends on word of mouth and informal friendships, which means that people who are different, and typically less known by those in positions of power, lose out. And the most challenging work assignments in some places continue to be given to men rather than women because those giving out the assignments have more friendships with men than with women in their organizations.

From Monocultural   **To Multicultural**

Exclusive Club	Lip Service to Inclusion	Tokenism	A Critical Mass	Tolerating/ Accepting Diversity	Valuing Diversity

Exclusive Organization   **Inclusive Organization**

Fig. 12.1 The Organizational Continuum

Organizations that are making rapid progress toward supporting diversity typically focus their change efforts on both individual and systemic change. What follows is an example that may help clarify the difference between working at the individual level and the systemic level.

EXAMPLE:

Marilyn Soto, a manager in the trust department of the Desert Bank in Phoenix, is concerned because one of the members of her workgroup, Jonathan, seems to be bored with his job and is making more mistakes than he used to. Each day at five o'clock he rushes out the door.

Individual-level solution: Jonathan is an employee whose performance is mediocre. His manager, Marilyn, sits down and has a conversation with him about his career—what part of his job does he enjoy, where does he hope to be in three years, and what does he need to do to get there? Marilyn is working at the *individual level*. She might discover, for example, that Jonathan is bored and wants more training. His lackluster performance may be the result of a lack of challenge.

Systemic Solutions:
1. After doing a bit of checking with others in her workgroup, Marilyn decides that there may be a more general problem here. So she sits down with each of the nine people in her workgroup and talks about their career development. Furthermore, she announces that every year she will sit down with each person for a similar conversation about career development and aspirations.
2. The head of Human Resources hears about Marilyn's plan for her workgroup. He thinks she has a great idea and is instrumental in developing a policy at Desert Bank that provides for annual career development conversations with every bank employee. Now everyone in the 3000-employee group will be affected by the change. Both of these are systemic changes—the first

changes the system at the workgroup level, whereas the second targets the whole organization, that is the entire system.

		Organizational Change	
		No	Yes
Individual Change	No	1 No change	2 Wasted systems Resistance
	Yes	3 Short-lived Cynicism	4 Enduring change Well supported

To be most effective and enduring, change needs to take place at both the individual level and the organizational level. A four-box model is useful in illustrating this point.

THE FOUR-BOX MODEL—AN ILLUSTRATION

A large city in the Midwest developed a new computerized reporting system for all its agencies at a cost of $1 million. It was difficult to understand, and none of the employees received any training in the system. This change effort falls into Box 2—there was an organizational change with no supporting individual change. The result: Over 90 percent of the agencies didn't implement the new tracking system and continued to report their statistics using the old paper forms. Thus, we see both resistance and a wasted system resulting from ignoring the individuals. (In this case, the city administration was so disorganized that it gave up on the system entirely.) In order to create enduring change (Box 4), the individual users of the new system would have needed significant training up front and ongoing support for several months.

Another Example

James Wellington, a manager in a small high-tech company, went to a training program called "Diversity Awareness." He got all fired up about diversity and came back to his workgroup full of enthusiasm. When he tried to explain about all he had learned, his coworkers told him to "get off his soap box." After being silenced three times, James said to himself, "They just don't get it." In terms of the model, this is a case of Box 3. There was change at the individual level, but none at the organizational level, and the change was short-lived. James soon completely forgot about diversity. For this change to be effective, it would have made more sense for the whole workgroup to attend the training program.

These two examples suggest that if you want to create changes that are enduring, it is important to work at *both* the individual *and* the systemic or organizational level.

Changing the Organization to Support Diversity
What Is Fair?

Here we move into one of the new paradoxes of the 1990s. Managers used to be trained that "fair is treating everyone exactly the same." Now a new, and in some ways contradictory, definition of fair has emerged alongside the old one: "Fair is providing support to all employees so that they can develop to their full potential and contribute fully to the organization." This may mean treating people in different circumstances differently. For example, a woman with a dying mother may need extra time off that no one else is getting. Or allowing a man to leave work early to attend a course at a nearby college may be key in keeping him from leaving the company for another job.

The Successful Diversity Initiative

To create an organization that truly supports diversity usually requires a multifaceted and carefully planned organizational change effort. We have learned that successful efforts begin in different places and that not all successful initiatives include exactly the same components. What is certain is that diversity work is not a single event but a process that requires several years and ongoing support.

THE ROLE OF THE CEO

Successful diversity efforts often begin when the CEO announces that diversity is one of his or her top priorities. This kind of support launches the change effort in a way that makes the whole organization take notice. Of course, the commitment needs to be more than lip service. The CEO needs to display a consistent commitment to diversity through many actions over a long period of time.

DEVELOPING THE VISION

A critical part of any diversity effort is creating a tangible vision of what valuing diversity means and how the truly multicultural organization looks. Over and over we hear employees asking for greater clarity about what their organization is planning and what it wants from them in terms of diversity. "What does our president really want for this organization?" they wonder. The way you get the troops all moving in the same direction is to clearly communicate the vision. What are the goals, the desired objectives, and what can each individual do to help?

STRATEGIC PLANS

Once the vision has been communicated, the organization needs a strategic plan that spells out how the organization will make the vision a reality. This plan can be developed by the CEO and his or her direct reports, with or without the help of diversity consultants. Another approach is to utilize a task force, a steering committee, or a diversity council. We have found that the more concrete the plan, the more likelihood there is of its being utilized as a road map in the months ahead. Be careful about losing momentum, however. Some organizations have spent years just developing the plan. This has created frustration on the part of their action-oriented employees and slowed down overall movement.

THE DIVERSITY AUDIT

Conducting a diversity audit is an excellent way to assess the present state of the organization and get the information necessary to develop a good plan. Audits may have three components:

1. A *document review*. This consists of reviewing annual reports, brochures, in-house newsletters, and key demographic statistics.

2. *A survey.* Often all employees or a sample of employees are surveyed. The goal of the survey is to learn how they perceive diversity in the organization and their beliefs about opportunities for themselves and others.
3. *Focus groups.* A focus group consists of four to twelve people and a facilitator who meet to discuss a specific topic. Focus groups, we believe, are the best way to get in-depth information about employees' experiences in the workplace. They also give information about the real impact of the corporate culture and the effects of organizational systems on diverse employees. Typically in our focus groups, we ask questions such as:

"What does it take to get ahead in this organization?"

"What is it like for you as a Hispanic, an African-American, a white male, or a woman to work in this organization?"

Focus groups work best when they are homogeneous, that is, made up of employees who are similar along a number of dimensions, such as gender, race, ethnicity, function, or level in the organization. The audit provides the organization with baseline data against which to measure future progress in creating a workplace environment in which diversity is valued. It also involves significant numbers of employees in the process and builds commitment to change.

DIVERSITY COUNCIL

A diversity council or diversity task force is an extremely effective way of creating momentum for diversity work and is a useful structure for managing the actual process. The council usually consists of ten to twenty-four employees from various levels of the organization and includes employees from diverse groups. We have found that it is particularly important to include a significant number of white men, particularly several senior-level white men.

Councils play a variety of roles, such as reviewing the data from an audit and creating a diversity strategic plan for the organization. They can also become the groups that create recommendations for change and track and recognize progress. In some cases, the councils actually implement some of the changes as well. In brief, the diversi-

ty council is typically the centerpiece for diversity action and a catalyst for organizational change.

ORGANIZATIONAL CHANGE—DOING IT

Often the organizational audit uncovers many areas and systems that
are not working as well as they could. It may reveal that the organization, despite the good intentions of almost everybody, does not provide a level playing field for all employees. All too often, once the
audit has been completed and a number of recommendations have
been generated, momentum gets lost. In some cases, things come to a
halt entirely and nothing more happens.

We have found from our consulting work that an active diversity council is the best way to ensure ongoing action and change.
Sometimes the council members themselves form action groups to
work on specific projects. Sometimes the recommendations are
made to the senior management team, that approves them and
assigns the task of getting projects done to the appropriate people in
the organization.

Here are examples of the kinds of changes/projects emerging
from diversity audits that have been implemented at organizations
where we have consulted:

- Benchmarking project to visit other pioneering companies to learn
  what they have done in terms of diversity
- Training for all employees in diversity awareness
- Development of a career development system
- Job data bank to provide larger candidate pools
- Internal job fair to help employees learn about career opportunities
  within the organization
- Development of a corporate policy on diversity
- Brochure written to bring together all the company's policies on
  work and family issues
- Broadened job posting system, including more levels
- Incorporating materials on diversity into all the management train-
  ing programs
- Introduction of a "Take Your Daughter to Work Day"
- Lunchtime seminars—programs on diversity issues held on a
  monthly basis

- Breakfast for employees to give input to senior management on a regular basis
- Introduction of permanent, part-time jobs with benefits, parental leave, and job sharing
- Change of separate sick days and vacation days into paid leave to allow parents with sick children to take time off without lying
- Development of a recruitment program using African-American and Hispanic line managers to assist in recruiting other people of color

DIVERSITY TRAINING

Often organizations begin their diversity work with a program on diversity awareness. These sessions range from three hours to five days, with most programs lasting a half day to a whole day. A typical design that we use looks like this:

Introductions
The Business Case for Diversity
Video: *A Class Divided*
The Dynamics of Discrimination and Difference
Reviewing the Data from the Organization's Focus Groups
Role Plays—Dealing With the Day-to-Day Dilemmas of Diversity
Speaking Up—Creating the Culture of Inclusion
Action Planning
- What I can do
- What I can do with my workgroup
- My advice for our CEO

After the initial awareness training, as organizations get really serious about their diversity work, they typically conduct additional training in managing diversity to help managers and supervisors deal with the challenges of the diverse workforce. Diversity involves skill training in areas such as "Understanding Our Own Cultural Biases," "Managing a Diverse Team," and "Communication Skills for the Multicultural Organization." Other more specialized programs offered are "Preventing Sexual Harassment," "Work and Family Issues," and "Leadership for Women." In the mid- and late 1990s, diversity training is getting more differentiated, as organizations see that awareness training is only the first in a long series of actions necessary to change the organizational systems culture.

NETWORKING GROUPS

Networking groups for women, Asian-Americans, African-Americans, Hispanics, and gays and lesbians have been formed in many large organizations across the country. Often these groups begin informally, meeting at a local lounge after hours. Sometimes they receive official sanction, along with budgets, and meet on work time.

Xerox, galvanized into action by a class action suit brought against the company by African-American employees in 1971, formed networking groups in the mid-1970s. The Black Caucus received significant support, although in the early years some people were concerned about its becoming a national association that could border on a trade union. The impact of the network has been to dramatically increase the numbers of black managers, an accomplishment that few other organizations have been able to match. The goal at Xerox has been a balanced workforce, a strategy aimed at correcting the problems associated with affirmative action, and a strategy that includes white males.

STUDY GROUPS

Digital Equipment Corporation's approach to diversity, called "Valuing Differences," used study groups as a vehicle for change. Core groups, as they were called, met for several hours a month on company time and helped members to explore all kinds of diversity issues, including their own stereotypes. Employees were encouraged to pay attention to their differences as individuals and as groups. The importance of dialogue was key, and the importance of learning from one another was emphasized.

Many DEC employees reported that their experience in a core group had a major impact on their life. As the company downsized in the 1990s, however, the core groups languished. Some participants have told us recently that although many individual employees were transformed by these groups, the basic organizational systems were left untouched. We have been told, "Knowing what I know now, I'd do it differently. We needed to change the system too."

MENTORING

Mentoring programs are a more controversial kind of diversity initiative. Typically a high-level manager or executive is paired with a lower-level manager, either a woman or a person of color, who is seen as a rising star. The purpose is to provide counsel, support, and information about the work culture to the younger manager. In practice, these programs have proved difficult to implement. When the program excludes white men, resistance is generated. Sometimes the matches between people aren't good. Most often, people just are too busy to follow through. Many such programs have withered away over time because of these and other difficulties.

RESISTANCE TO CHANGE

Diversity work is difficult. Changing the culture and practices of an organization is always complicated, and the process takes years. Bringing in new kinds of people can be threatening. This is normal, to be expected as part of any change process. The amount of resistance may be truly surprising. What is critical for success is for the organization to build structures for keeping the work going, for tracking progress, and for continuing, in spite of this resistance.

It is important to bring the resistance to the surface and honor it. Do what you can to legitimize people's expressing their views honestly, no matter how much you disagree with them. Expressing their resistance to change is one step in allowing people to accept the change eventually.

We feel that the secret of success for diversity work (or any organizational change, for that matter) is using a participative process. Edgar Schein of the Sloan School of Management at MIT puts it this way, "The job…is to help the organization to solve its own problems by making it aware of organizational processes, the consequences of these processes, and the mechanisms by which they can be changed."[2] That quote sums up our fundamental strategy.

ACCOUNTABILITY

Diversity work usually falters because the organization has failed to build accountability into its diversity initiatives. There can be changes in top organizational priorities. There may be a downsizing or a reengineering effort. The CEO may leave. All of these are potential threats to ongoing process. Ann Morrison, in *The New Leaders, Guidelines on Leadership Diversity in America*,[3] lists twenty-three strate-

---

[2] Edgar H. Schein, *Process Consultation*, Vol. 1, Reading MA: Addison-Wesley, 1988; p. 193.

[3] Ann M. Morrison, *The New Leaders, Guidelines on Leadership Diversity in America*, San Francisco: Jossey-Bass Publishers, 1992; p. 294.

gies that can ensure accountability practices that keep up momentum. The top ten practices, ranked by importance, are listed below:

1. Top management's personal intervention
2. Internal advocacy groups
3. Emphasis on EEO statistics and profiles
4. Inclusion of diversity in performance evaluation goals and ratings
5. Inclusion of diversity in promotion decisions and criteria for such decisions
6. Inclusion of diversity in management succession planning
7. Work and family practices
8. Policies against racism and sexism
9. Internal audit or attitude survey
10. Active AA/EEO committee or office

A Final Note

We do think that change initiated by the organization is enormously important. In the final analysis, however, any change of an organizational culture or practice depends on employees at all levels changing the way they behave. The president of Scandinavian Airlines, who led a major transformation of his organization in the 1980s, remarked that organizational change does not depend on one thing being done 100 percent better but on one thousand things being done 1 percent better. We agree.

Each of you can make a difference. Each of you can help create a better workplace in which diversity is valued and all employees can develop to their fullest potential.

A P P E N D I C E S

APPENDIX A

GENERAL REFERENCES ON WORKPLACE DIVERSITY

BOOKS

John P. Fernandez, *The Diversity Advantage: How American Business Can Out-perform Japanese and European Companies in the Global Marketplace*, New York: Lexington Books, 1993.

Lee Gardenswartz and Anita Rowe, *Managing Diversity: A Complete Desk Reference and Planning Guide*, Homewood, IL: Business One Irwin, 1993.

Mary C. Gentile, ed., *Differences that Work: Organizational Excellence through Diversity*, Boston: Harvard Business School Publications, 1994.

Lawrence Otis Graham, *The Best Companies for Minorities*, New York: A Plume Book, 1993.

Susan E. Jackson and Associates, ed., *Diversity in the Workplace: Human Resources Initiatives*, New York: Guilford Press, 1992.

David Jameson and Julie O'Mara, *Managing Workforce 2000: Gaining the Diversity Advantage*, San Francisco: Jossey-Bass, 1991.

S. Kanu Kogod, *A Workshop for Managing Diversity in the Workplace*, San Diego: Pfeiffer & Co., 1991.

Marilyn Loden and Judith Rosener, *Workforce America: Managing Workforce Diversity as a Vital Resource*, Homewood, IL: Business One Irwin, 1991.

Craig Storti, *Cross-Cultural Dialogues: 74 Brief Encounters with Cultural Difference*, Intercultural Press, Inc., P.O. Box 7000, Yarmouth, ME 04096; (207) 846-5186, 1994.

Sondra Thiederman, Ph.D., *Bridging Cultural Barriers for Corporate Success: How to Manage the Multicultural Work Force*, Lexington, MA: Lexington Books, 1990.

Roosevelt R. Thomas, *Beyond Race and Gender: Unleashing the Power of Your Total Workforce by Managing Diversity*, New York: AMA-COM, 1991.

NEWSLETTERS

Cultural Diversity at Work, 13751 Lake City Way N.E., Suite 106, Seattle, WA 98125-3615; (206) 362-0336.

Cultural Etiquette: A Guide for the Well-Intentioned, Amoja Three Rivers ($5 from Market Wimmin, Box 28, Indian Valley, VA, 24105).

Managing Diversity, P.O. Box 819, Jamestown, NY 14702-0819; (800) 542-7869.

PERIODICALS

Extend: Multicultural Magazine: Diversity Views for Business Professionals (quarterly), P.O. Box 124783, San Diego, CA 92112-4783; (619) 236-0624.

OTHER PUBLICATIONS

Harris Sussman Answers Questions about Diversity, 1993, $12 from Diversity University, 57 Henry Street, Cambridge, MA 02139; (617) 876-3599.

HR Best Practices, Annual Reports. HR Effectiveness, Inc.; 16360 Southwest Cinnabar Court, Beaverton, OR, 97007; (503) 579-2727.

ARTICLES

Lisa Jenner, "Diversity Management: What Does It Mean?" *HR Focus*, January 1994, vol. 71, no. 1, p. 11.

Don McNerny, "The Bottom-Line Value of Diversity," *HR Focus*, May 1994, vol. 71, no. 5, p. 22.

Sharon Nelton, "Winning with Diversity" (includes directory of sources of information about diversity management in the workplace), *Nation's Business* (cover story), September 1992.

Judith Palmer, "Diversity: Three Paradigms for Change Leaders," *O.D. Practitioner, The Journal of the O.D. Network*, March 1989.

AUDIOVISUALS

The following are available from Video Learning, 230 Western Ave., Boston, MA 02134; (800) 225-3959:

The Diversity Series: Race, Ethnicity, Language, and Religion Workplace Issues, Quality Media Resources.

Harness the Rainbow, a motivational/training video series on diversity and change featuring Dr. Samuel Betances. Determan Marketing, and United Training Media.

Jack Cade's Nightmare: A Supervisor's Guide to Laws Affecting the Workplace, from BNA Communications; (800) 233-6067.

Managing Diversity, Carlsbad, CA: CRM Films.

Valuing Diversity, (7-part video), San Francisco: Copeland Griggs Productions.

The Power of Diversity: Creating Success for Business and People, CorVision Media, 1359 Barclay Blvd., Buffalo Grove, IL 60089; (800) 537-3130.

STRUCTURED EXERCISES

Bafá Bafá: Cross Cultural Orientation Exercises, Simulation Training Systems, P.O. Box 910, Del Mar, CA 92014; (619) 755-0272.

Barnga: A Simulation Game on Cultural Clashes, Intercultural Press, P.O. Box 700, Yarmouth, ME 04096.

APPENDIX **B**

IBIS GLOSSARY
OF DIVERSITY TERMS

AFFIRMATIVE ACTION: Government guidelines that set goals for the hiring and upward mobility of people of color and women based upon the difference between the availability of these groups in the population and their actual representation in the company (companies with government contracts must take affirmative action to hire such employees).

AGEISM: Prejudice or discrimination against a particular age group, usually the very young or the elderly.

ANTI-SEMITISM: Oppression of, or prejudice against, Jewish people.

ASSIMILATION: Being absorbed into the culture of an existing group in the workplace, conforming to the dominant culture of the organization.

BIAS: A distortion of judgment, prejudice.

BISEXUAL: Open to sexual relationships with persons of either sex.

CLASSISM: Attitude or prejudice on the basis of socioeconomic status.

CORPORATE CULTURE: A system of informal rules that spell out how people are to behave; the assumptions, practices, values, and taken-for-granted ways of seeing the world.

DISABILITY: A major physical or mental impairment.

DISCRIMINATION: Behavior or actions toward a person based on prejudice.

DIVERSITY: Differences among people, including age, ability or disability, and sexual orientation.

EQUAL EMPLOYMENT OPPORTUNITY: The legal requirement that all persons, regardless of race, sex, color, national origin, religion, age, ancestry, disability, marital status, medical condition, or sexual orientation, have equal opportunity in the areas of hiring, promotion, and all terms and conditions of employment.

EQUITY: Dealing fairly with all concerned, without bias or favoritism.

GAY: A term usually applied to men who have their primary emotional/sexual relationships with other men. This term is also used for lesbians.

HOMOPHOBIA: Fear, dislike, or disgust of homosexuality or homosexuals.

HOSTILE ENVIRONMENT: One of the two types of sexual harassment claims; requires a showing of frequent, nontrivial acts of a sexual nature that have the effect of creating a hostile, offensive, or intimidating working atmosphere.

LESBIAN: The term most preferred by women who form their primary emotional/sexual relationships with other women.

MELTING POT: The traditional assumption that foreigners in the United States should assimilate into the mainstream culture.

MULTICULTURAL ORGANIZATION: An organization whose employees are of notably different cultural and ethnic backgrounds, races, genders, etc.

PLURALISM: An organization or society in which members of diverse ethnic, racial, religious, or social groups maintain their own culture and traditions and in which differences are valued.

PREJUDICE: An evaluative reaction (usually negative) to a member of a racial, ethnic, or other group that results primarily from the person's membership in that group.

RACISM: The belief that one group of people are superior to others and therefore have the right to dominate.

SEX DISCRIMINATION: The favoring of one individual or gender over another; behavior favoring one gender or the other.

SEXISM: Stereotyping of males and females on the basis of gender, particularly the oppression of women.

SEXUAL HARASSMENT: Unwelcome sexual conduct toward an employee in the workplace through which sexual favors are demanded or a hostile environment is created.

SOCIAL SIMILARITY SYNDROME: The widespread tendency for people to hire and promote persons similar to themselves along gender, racial, and ethnic dimensions.

STEREOTYPE: A relatively rigid and oversimplified conception of a group of people in which individuals in the group are assumed to have similar characteristics.

T H E   A U T H O R S

Katharine Esty, Ph.D. is President of Ibis Consulting Group, Inc., a management consulting firm based in Cambridge, Massachusetts that specializes in diversity and the management of change. A social psychologist by training, she describes herself as a lifelong change agent. Over the last fifteen years she has consulted to a wide variety of organizations including Navistar, Gillette, Chevron, Massachusetts General Hospital, The Unitarian Universalist Association, Boston Gas Company, Tungsram, AT&T, The Appalachian Mountain Club, State Street Bank and Trust, Data General and Lesley College. Currently, Katharine's work is focusing on helping organizations manage the increasingly diverse workforce and to develop corporate initiatives to support diversity.

Marcie Schorr Hirsch is a career development and management expert who lectures, writes, and consults on work issues. She has directed the Career Centers at both Wellesley College and Brandeis University, has co-authored several books on workplace topics and writes regularly for the popular press. Marcie is a frequent communicator on career and work issues on local and national radio and television; she has also served as writer and executive producer for several videos on work and careers, including "The Recruiting Game" and "Good Job" as well as broadcast programs titled "The Good News About Being Fired" and "Dream Jobs." Marcie holds a doctorate from the Harvard Graduate School of Education.

Richard Griffin, columnist, educator, and consultant, specializes on diversity issues, especially those involving older workers and people with disabilities. He often lectures on these topics to students as well as presenting workshops to industry and not for profit organizations. An alumnus of Harvard College, Richard has written handbooks and many other materials for business. For several years he has appeared on public television in Boston. A former university chaplain, Richard has a continuing interest in religious issues, spiritual matters, and ethical questions.